Austin Mitchell's

Grand
book of
YORKSHIRE
HUMOUR

Foreword
by Ian McMillan
Yorkshire Poet Laureate

GREAT-N-ORTHERN

Great Northern Books
PO Box 213, Ilkley, LS29 9WS
www.greatnorthernbooks.co.uk

ISBN: 978 1 905080 64 9

Design and layout: David Burrill

Printed in China

CIP Data
A catalogue for this book is available from the British Library

Foreword

by Ian McMillan

Our old Latin teacher Mr Dunsby at Wath Grammar School near Rotherham was a nice guy but he wasn't very good at jokes; the nearest he got was a chant that he swore was hilarious. It was in Latin (of course) and it went *Caesar adrarat forte; Brutus adsum jam. Ceasar sic in Omnibus; Brutus sic intram.* I think you have to say it aloud to make it work properly. Anyway, he enjoyed wit, old Mr Dunsby: rumour had it that he subscribed to Punch and The New Yorker and cut the cartoons out and stuck them in the book. Us fifteen-year-olds tried to keep up with him, tried to engage him in discussions about who was the greatest comic writer, SJ Perelman or James Thurber.

One day one of the lads brought in Austin Mitchell's book of Yorkshire Jokes and Mr Dunsby did an unusual thing: he bowed. Mr Dunsby was as tall as a lamp post and could be seen from passing planes, so him bowing was quite a sight. He spoke, his voice muffled because he was bowing. *This man is a genius* he said, his face going puce as the blood

3

rushed from the far regions of his legs. *He is a bona fide comic genius.* Austin Mitchell: comic genius. I think you'll agree when you've read this book, and once you've taken note of the fact that even when he was praising somebody Mr Dunsby couldn't help speaking Latin.

Let's face it: people from Yorkshire aren't that easy to impress. Mr Dunsby never laughed much, even when he was discussing wit, but he said that Austin Mitchell genuinely made him laugh. I once performed my 'humorous' poetry at a Working Mens' Club in Doncaster in the days when there were enough working men in Doncaster to form a club. Everywhere else in the UK people had laughed at my poems. Or at least they'd chuckled. Or smiled. At the end of my set, a man came up to me. He was the polar opposite of Mr Dunsby, short and squat. 'I've seen some bad turns in my time,' he said, 'but tha were't worst. If a bobby came in he'd summons thi.' His mate, who looked like a garden gnome, said, 'Tha norras funny as Austin' and everybody in the club knew what he meant.

Our motto at Wath Grammar was a Latin one: *Meliora Spectare*. Mr Dunsby told us it meant Look to better things and I know the better things he meant: Austin Mitchell, comic genius. Salute!

t'intoduction

Na then thee.

These Yorkshire Jokes are guaranteed fully organic. They are the natural product of free-range Yorkshire folk living naturally and free within the bounds of Britain`s biggest, best, and most beautiful county, the one whose National Airways, Air Yorkshire as well as Tyke Tours and Beautyke Holidays, all went bankrupt because they could find nowhere nicer to fly to.

They come out of Yorkshire`s native heath and hill, mine and mill, evolved not made, and not coming from any joke production factory or from overpaid script writers: we don`t need to pay them here. Every Yorkshireman`s his own joke writer and each has a full file of them in his head – so when you see a Tyke sitting with lips moving but no mobile phone you'll know he's committing them to memory. The jokes are handed down from father to son (and occasionally daughter) neither invented nor cleaned up by clever clogs in London. They are also entirely natural (though not pure) containing no added colour, flavouring or preservative. They have developed for our taste, not yours. So they`re not politically correct either. That`s a concept for namby pambies, not real Yorkshire folk who once knew well that a woman`s place is on her back, or in the scullery, or both. As it always has been. So our only defence to the PC Plague is that we don't say "there's nowt so queer as folk" any more. But we still

Ask a Yorkshireman how he is and he'll either say nowt or,
if he's really happy, he'll tell you things could be worse.

think it. Particularly about some folk.

Yorkshire`s taste in humour is a natural phenomenon. Just like those other natural phenomena: sex (natural variety only), death (ditto), diareah (ditto) and drink, which give us what little pleasure we admit to. The best of our Yorkshire traditions are those which produce most jokes. They have never been set down before, except on the walls of lavatories in Bradford now pulled down because they`re an oral tradition meant for Yorkshiremen to savour, though never to laugh at. They are being made available now to you but only on the strict understanding that they are kept out of sight of minors, professional comedians, pushy women, politically correct effetists, and any other groups incapable of appreciating their full subtlety.

You can always tell a Yorkshireman, though not much. You tell him mainly by his deeply miserable mein which is different to mean, though he`s that too. Being Yorkshire is no laughing matter. My wife claims, in her whinging woman's way, that it's worse for Yorkshirewomen than it is for the men who grace them with their affections, but not having been born Tyke she's wrong. As usual. To live with a Yorkshireman, to serve, cook and clean for him and to breed his Yorkshire children is the greatest happiness, and the most fulfilling role any woman can have. We`re a race apart because Yorkshiremen have a higher destiny, a more serious role and a greater responsibility than any of the lesser breeds without the county. As humanity's finest flowering, we're Britain's best breeding stock, living on its biggest and best stud farm. These jokes embody the philosophy that has made us grate. On everybody. Not that we`re miserable. Just realistic. As the Driffield hypochondriac's tombstone put it, "Ah tell`t thi ah wor proper poorly".

We're a Big Nation bred big to fill the space of Britain's, nay the world's biggest county placed where it is by God to be looked up to by the huddled masses south of the border. So an enormous responsibility rests on broad Yorkshire shoulders. We're serious folk. It`s a serious job living up to our role, standing ever ready to serve, to save the rest of the world from themselves and to offer it a little friendly advice on an unpaid basis about how stupid it`s been and is being. We can`t do anything to eliminate their great disadvantage of not being born in the Broad Acres. Yet we can help them a little bit by giving them our jokes to brighten their misery at not being born Yorkshire.

Our jokes. Not our laughter. To laugh is to give summat away. We're not much inclined to do that. Not that we're mean, though it was known that fowk in terrace houses who wanted to gas theirselves would break through into next door to do it, and the difference between a tightrope and a Yorkshireman is that a tightrope sometimes gives. Every Yorkshire cop knows that the best way to disperse an angry Yorkshire crowd is to take a collection and if we do give owt it`s always calculated on a return, like the Holmfirth housewife offering her friend a slice of cake. "No thanks" came the reply. "Ah`ve `ad two already!" "Nay, tha`s `ad four but tha`s welcome to another". So you can`t and mustn`t laugh at a Yorkshireman if you value your teeth. You could laugh with him but since he doesn't, you`ll be laughing alone. So just laugh at his jokes. They're the best in the world and you`ll be expected to point that out with due gratitude. But never expect us to laugh at them or at your own pathetic humour. Above all give nowt away. The

Yorkshire answer to the question "Could you pass me the sugar?" is "Aye". Followed by inert silence. "Will tha?" is another matter.

We have brilliant jokes but we aren't a race of comedians. Comedians come from Liverpool where there's more to laugh at and lots of Lancashire chancers trying to make the best of their natural disadvantages. By contrast, we specialise in misery. So Yorkshire is a professional comedian's graveyard. Sir Henry Irving died on stage in Bradford and generations of comedian's have followed him. Both Ken Dodd and Harry Secombe reported giving their all to apparently dead Yorkshire audiences getting no reaction, but being approached afterwards by some taciturn and naturally blunt speaking Tyke saying "tha war reet funny ter neet. Ah almost 'ad to laugh at some of thi jokes". He didn't of course. That's not a Yorkshire job. Ours is to brood on fate and the sins of the world, outside the Broad Acres, not to giggle at trivia.

Humour can be safely left to Londoners, like laugh a minute East Enders, or to Lancastrians who've nothing better to do. We Yorkshirefolk have to look on the black side and there we always derive great satisfaction from the fact that it could be worse. Ask a Yorkshireman how he is and he'll either say nowt or, if he's really happy, he'll tell you things could be worse. That means he's doing fantastically well and is positively ecstatic at living in Britain's best, biggest and most beautiful county.

However, he's not prepared to show that to you nor share it with you. So he won`t tell you about his happiness in case you come and try to share it by living it up here, too, and making the place overcrowded.

It`s not a cheerful job being a Yorkshireman. We`re always aware what "worse" is because it`s always hovering over us and could hit us hard at any moment. Indeed, it probably will if we attract it by a welcoming smile. If everything's coming towards a Yorkshireman then he knows he's in the wrong lane. If its coming up roses he's planted orchids. If life's a bowl of cherries, they'll give him stomach ache. Look on the bright side in Yorkshire and it's clear you need glasses. Even if the worst doesn't always happen there's pleasure in anticipating it in advance, savouring the fact that it might hit someone else and then exuding relief that it's not quite that bad for you when it does. If you have an accident the maximum comfort and support Yorkshire folk will give you is saying "Could be worse. Tha` could be dead". How true.

Our proverbs are different to everyone else's. "One door closes. Another door slams". "Red sky at night a mill owner's delight". He`s probably burned it down to collect the insurance in the best Bradford tradition. "Think small ant' big'll tek care of itssen". "When tha`s down there`s nowhere to go but further down". "Expect to lose an' tha'll not be disappointed", a particularly useful proverb when thinking of the County Cricket team in the space since Fred Truman and Geoff Boycott gave up and before Darren Gough came along, or for fans of Halifax Town and Wakefield Trinity. Yorkshire`s support for any of its teams is always alloyed by the certainty that opponents will cheat, the referee will lose his white stick or the heavens will open and it'll be siling i' stair rods, just as a Yorkshire team is poised to win. There's no situation so bad that it can't be made worse by a few well chosen Yorkshire words or by the glum expressions on Yorkshire faces. As a race we make wonderful undertakers. Though sadly not very good at comforting the bereaved. The deceased probably had it coming to him anyway.

Life's hard in Yorkshire and we Tykes have been hardened by it. We`ve developed the understanding that there's no use laughing at fate because it will get its own back. So why not savour the simple pleasures of misery. Then if anything better comes along it's an improvement. You've got to be stoical in a county whose sheep scrounge enough nourishment from barren hillsides to keep them going until they're slaughtered for foot and mouth, where textile workers struggle for a living on low pay in outdated mills always on the brink of closure, or farmers spend years building dry stone walls up hillsides Edmund Hillary couldn't climb, just to show who belongs it.

Centuries of struggle have made Yorkshirefolk hard but realistic and our jokes are both. Most are about the pleasure of sheer, simple misery of the kind you only get in Yorkshire. Tha` goes on Ilkla Moor not to enjoy its splendid scenery but to get thi` death o' cold. Then us all 'ave t' pleasure of burying and eventually eating thee. Was there ever a more miserable national anthem even in Rwanda. Let`s face it, fellow Tykes we`re never happier than when:

> *We're all dahn int' coil-oil*
> *Weer t'muck slahts ont' winders*
> *We've burnt all us coil*
> *And we're agate burning t'cinders*
> *When t'bumbailiffs come*
> *They'll nivver find us*

Cos we're all dahn in t'coil oil
Weer t'much slahts onto'winders

Sadly, Yorkshrie jokes don't travel well. They're not like our Millstone grit from pulled down mills and back-to-backs or, stolen cars, or Yorkshire furniture and all our other antiques; summat tha` can take down to London and flog at a profit. Nor are our jokes there to produce great roars of laughter. In Yorkshire laughter is a sign of weakness, possibly mental deficiency and we're not in the habit of giving owt away. Not even laughter, though it isn't true that a Yorkshireman wouldn't give you a light if thi trousers were on fire. He'd certainly offer advice, perhaps tell you what was happening and derive a quiet pleasure from it. Have you heard the one about a Yorkshireman who gave away £1000 from his lottery winnings? No, neither have I. Indeed a Yorkshire lottery winner will never tell anyone he's won it. Not because of the threat of begging letters. He'll still keep sending them. It`s because so many people will want to share the winnings and his Income Support could even be stopped. Remember the advert in the Craven Herald "For Sale. Second hand gravestone. Suit anyone called Amos Arkroyd".

The happiest Yorkshire stories all end in rigor mortis; even in a more serious form of retribution:

Joah Jolly bowt a fahry 'oss
It cost him fifty pounds
One fine day ee went away
To 'ave an hunt wi' t'ounds
First fence Joah cum to

Joah Jolly bowt a fahry 'oss...

Ee sez "Nah Lad Goah"
Ee cleared that fence
Wi'out 'is 'oss
An' that were t'end on Joah.

Some labour under the mistaken impression that Yorkshire jokes are all about Lancastrians, their lack of intelligence, their inability to play cricket, their hob-gobian stupidity. Far from it. These are mere statements of fact. We don't wish Lancastrians any ill they haven't done to themselves already. It would be absolutely wrong to say that the only good Lancastrian is a dead one as some used to. That may be true of Southerners, hence the joke "What do you call 500 southerners drowned in't'Thames? A good start" because southerners are so cold and clammy they suffer from premature rigor mortis, but not Lancastrians. Living in that benighted county is probably worse than death anyway.

No, our jokes are about ourselves. They're the essence of us and of Yorkshire. They're not modern but traditional, not quickfire but cryptic, not satirical but realistic, not topical but eternal, not abstruse but basic. These are jokes of, for, and by the people, folk jokes, nothing to do with professional comedians (who have to be paid) and they're basic because Yorkshire is the land of basic realities. So basic that our jokes mostly revolve round the absolute basics of death, disease, defeats at cricket, diarrhoea, debt, depression and the dole, all the things, in short, which make and keep us happy. The great archetypes our jokes deal with are on the eight Ds. Nine if you add t'dales:

Category One. Death

Death comes to us all, even to Yorkshirefolk, so being a bit Methodistical we're reverential towards it. But as Canon the Rt. Rev. Bert Smith of Bradford Cathedral puts it "In us beginning is us end and in us end is us jokes" (sermon on Shipley Glen). The jokes mostly begin with an old bloke, trudging down a long terrace of back-to-back houses. At the very last door he stops, knocks and is greeted by a sobbing widow. "Ello Mrs. Is Fred in?" "Nay Ees dead. Took reet sudden in't neet. Ahm just waiting for t'undertaker". "Ee Mrs. Ahm reet sorry to 'ear that". Pause for thought and as much sympathy as she's going to get. "Did ee say owt about a pot o'paint?"

Category Two. Disease   (Preferably Diarrhoea)

Sam goes t'doctor. "Can tha give us summat ter mek us costive bound?" ee sez. "Ah've got awful diarrhoea."

"Sorry to hear that, "sez t'doctor. "How long have you had it?"

"Ah don't reetly know," sez Sam. "Ah didn't find out till I took mi bicycle clips off."

Category Three. Dialect

It`s nice to be able to get a quiet revenge by speaking to the foreigners who come North to discover the source of the M1 in God`s Own Language. They talk down to us but don`t even bother to buy a phrase book to talk reet.

Visitor arrives in Bradford. Wanting a local paper ee sez to t'lad, "I can't remember the one I enjoyed last time. But I know it started with a T."

"Tha'daft bugger," sez t'lad. "They all do. There's t'Telegraph, t'Argus and t'Observer."

Category Four. Dog Dirt

Except in effete Harrogate this isn't a pooper scooper county. Nor can it be stamped out by giving our dogs constipation awareness training. So dog dirt is something we face down to boldy as we march where southerners fear to tread. "Dad, sitha yon dog 'umping us Rover like ee war a wheelbarra'," sez t'little lad. Is Father belts im to teach 'im some manners. "Ow many times 'ave I telt thee not ter say 'sitha'."

Category Five. Defeats at Cricket

Sadly more common than they used to be with a particularly large crop after the departure of Close, Illingworth, Trueman and Boycott – all gone but not forgotten. Or forgiven come to that. But here`s a sample which predates that.

Yorkshire are in difficulties at Bramhall Lane. The world's best bowlers can make no impression on Lancashire. The restive crowd shouts advice, "Put Fred on." After a time, "Put Ray on." Despairingly, "Put thissen on Close." Finally, and with more feeling, "Put t'clock on. Then we can all gerrome."

Category Six. Depression

Not the psychological state which is congenital but the economic misery of days when we 'ad to wipe the sweat off us brows wi' t`slack of us bellies. Unlike those parts of the country which had a far easier time than Yorkshire in the great depression or during Mrs Thatcher's DIY re-enactments of it, we enjoyed our depression. It was being so miserable that kept us going through the dark days. So every Yorkshireman has jokes about how poor and tough life was, even in Harrogate, how tea leaves got eighteen mashes to drain every last drop of flavour and folk stood around waiting for a cat to be run over for dinner. Even now where life is at its most depressed in council estates where car wheels get stolen if they slow down to thirty, dustbins have to be padlocked, and you can guarantee on Hull`s Orchard Estate that if your video is stolen you`ll be offered it back after a few weeks, it's the jokes that get pawned last. Like the one about the Quick Confession system introduced in Leeds to deal with shop-lifting by having boxes for three sins or less.

Category Seven. Debt

A natural condition in the land that invented the Provident Cheque, the Fifty Shilling Tailors, the building society and brought the joys of the mail order catalogue to its highest form. We spend cautiously because we've nowt and its necessary to look as if we `aven`t in case the dole office, the Revenue, the Tally man or the rent officer tries to get summat out of us. Like the little girl getting her mother's order from t`Co-op. Included in it was a most unusual item, a toilet roll, largely unknown in a county where orange wrappers and the Yorkshire Post were better designed for the job. "We're 'aving company", she explained. But next day she was back at the Co-op with her toilet roll asking for her money back, "T'company didn't cum".

Category Eight. Dole

Why do they call Barnsley t`laike district?  `Cos there`s that many on`t`dole.

Back in Mrs. Thatcher`s golden days when queues outside every Job Centre were worse ner than for Bradford Northern in 1947 when they wun t`League Cup, two nuns broke down driving past the Dodworth Dole Centre. A friendly Tyke wandered over and offered to repair the engine if one of the nuns would keep his place in the long queue. She did. After half an hour another P45er joining the queue saw the nun and nudged his mate. "Bloody hell! It`s so bad now even t`Pope`s laying em off!"

Category Nine. Dales

The frontier is America`s sustaining myth, the Dales ours. Every Yorkshireman is a Dalesman at heart which is why so many used to have allotments to recreate the joys of Dales farming before their ancestors were driven off by enclosures. Today most allotments have reverted to nature, as our contribution to restoring the damage done by the destruction of the Amazonian tropical rain forest. Yet we still make regular pilgrimages to the Dales and get back to nature by winding our car windows down to get the freshest fresh air available in Britain, while swapping Dales jokes, like "Ow dos ter like living I`Grassington?"  "Eee, it`s a bit noisy after Uberholme".

Or

Owd Dalesman o` 82.  Goes t`t`doctor i`Thwaites for t`furst time.  "Ah`ve cum becos ah`ve got toilet problems.

Ah can`t go when ah want ter go!!" "Well, let`s take it step by step" says the doctor. "First, how`s your urination?" "Wot`s that?" "Pissing. Can you pee?" "Oh aye, ivery morn at seven. Just like a baby". "Excellent. Now what about your bowels?" "Oh aye. Ivery morn at eight. Like clockwork". "Well then, what`s your problem? It all looks OK to me". "But ah don`t wek up til nine these days".

That's it. That's us. Love us or gerr'ome.

US JOKES

GERRONWI'EM

Up Mount Tabor, Will Aspinall loses his wife of fifty years. Determined to give her the best possible funeral money can buy, he hires the best stone mason around with the highest charges per ton of headstone. Will desperately wants a message that sums up his loving wife and her religious devotion. After a long agony he decides that the text should read "Lord She Was Thine". "Bloody Ummer that's brilliant" say all t`fowks. So ee tells t`monumental mason and after weeks of carving and chipping there's a little ceremony round the grave to unveil the stone. Shock! Horror! It's revealed to read: "Lord She was Thin". "Yer daft bugger. Tha`s missed t`bloody E." says the grieving widower. Abject grovelling apologies from the stonemason. The stone is carted off to be recarved ready for a new ceremony. Again, the family stand around. Again the hymns are sung. Again the cover falls. To reveal "Ee Lord She was Thin."

Electricution teachers want us to talk like we don`t. Like the keen new teacher in Sheffield teaching her class the proper use of words.

"Now class," she sez, "I`d like you to make a sentence using the word `Charming`". The first girl to put her hand up

"Ee Lord She was Thin!"

said "A young man held the door open for us and mummy said he was charming".

The next little boy just said "Pregnant". "But, Arthur", said the teacher, "that`s nothing to do with charming". "Yes it `as, Miss. When us sister told me dad she war pregnant ee said, `Charming. Bloody charming`".

"Marvellous stuff this snuff!"

Alone up Claremount on t' hillside above Halifax where all t' houses have been pulled down sits this old pub. No-one much goes to it now except a few old blokes who keep coming to get the free snuff provided after every pint. New landlord takes over and decides that snuff is too expensive. It has to go to save the pub. Instead he dries and grinds up horse manure to replace it.

Next night t`first old bloke comes, has `is pint, teks `is snuff. "Ell`s bells, there`s a smell of shit in `ere". "I can`t smell owt" says the landlord. Next old bloke comes in. "Can ter smell t` shit, Fred?" "Nay". Well `ave some o`this 'ere snuff. It`ll sharpen thi` nose". "Bloody `ell, tha`s reet. Marvellous stuff this snuff. Ah`d nivver a` smelled t`shit t`new landlord`s brought in wi`out it".

Ventriloquist going from pub to pub int`remote Dales decides to mek a bob or two from gullible farmers. At the first remote farm he tells t`gaffer "I can talk to trees and animals". "Nivver". "Well let`s ask that tree. Do you like it here?" T`tree replies "Well, it`s bloody cold in winter but t`farmer`s all reet". "Bloody ell" sez t`farmer. "Let`s have a word with your dog. How do you like the farmer?" "Oh, ee`s a grand lad". At that moment a sheep wanders into the yard. "Let`s ask the sheep. Hey sheep. How do you like the farmer?" The farmer grabs the sheep, slaps his hand over its mouth and tells it "Tha` mun`t`tell this bastard owt".

Don`t think that Southerners never come North. A lot come to Wakefield. One ot`best jails int`country. Jaspar St. John-Fotheringay-Smyth came up there for twenty years . To pass t`time ee decides to train a couple o`fleas ont`mattress (last man in war also from t`South). "Wonderful way of passing the time and I`ll make my fortune when I get out." For twenty year ee trained `is fleas to do all sorts o`fantastic tricks.

Then ee war released an goes down t`t`Dolphin for a pint. Ee can`t wait to show `is wonderful fleas. Gets out `is matchbox. Puts em ont`counter. Sez t`t`barman, "Tell me potman. Have you ever seen anything like this before?" Bartender crashes is `and down ont`fleas. "Aye, we get too many o`them damn things `ere".

What dos`ta call a beautiful woman int`Dales? "A tourist".

Before t`miners strike they worshipped Arthur Scargill as King Arthur in the Socialist State of South Yorkshire. A newly arrived Primary School teacher was shocked when she took Religious Instruction and asked the class "Children. Who made the world?" Back came the answer from all of them, "Miss, Arthur Scargill med t`world". "Don`t be silly, children. You know very well it was God who made the world". From the back of the class came the murmur "Bloody Tory".

Ethel takes little Sykes to the doctors. He hasn`t been to the lavatory in three days and she`s very worried. "Wot`s up wi im, Doc? Eee `asn`t bin for days. "Well, madam," replies the doctor. "I`m afraid he`s Costive Bound." "Ah don`t care if it costs two pund. Mek `im go".

Owd Amos, who`s lived in his tiny Dales cottage for seventy years has finally to sell it and to go to live int'owd folks 'ome. The first purchasers to arrive with a view to buy it are a young couple looking for a weekend holiday home. They`re full of admiration for the cottage. "What lovely beams – what a marvellous view – we love that open range". Finally the husband asks where the toilet is. "It`s down t`yard. It`s a double necessire. Tha can sit and shit an` `old `ands" "But there`s no lock on the door" the husband says as he emerges. "Don`t worry thissen. Ah`v lived `ere seventy years and no-one`s stolen so much as a turd yet".

A Special Constable, used to weighty responsibilities, is going home off duty but comes across a crowd of kids fighting to get on the school special bus. He`s horrified to see kids of different races all thumping each other in a mini race war "Stop. This is awful. We should all love each other, whatever the colour of our skins" he shouts. "Stop it! Stop it! Stop the fighting!". Gradually silence falls and the Special carefully explains that the different racial groups must all learn to live together. "Why not" he clutches at an illustration. "Why not think of yourselves not as brown or white, but as green. All of us. Green together". Shamed silence. The children are deeply moved and ashamed of themselves. The Special has won the day. He drives the lesson home. "Now children, I want you all to get on the bus in an orderly manner. Let the light greens get on first. Then the dark greens".

Ah thowt ah might go an` see a match at `Alifax Town t`other week. Just for old times` sake. So ah rang t`ground.

"What time`s t`kick off?" ah sez. "What time can yer get `ere," sez t`voice at t`other end. When ah did get there ah `ad to shake `ands wit`team an` they announced t`crowd changes t`t`team. Mark you, some kids were caught climbing t`wall. But they were made to go back and watch t`game.

"Doctor tha`s got to gi us summat ter lower mi sex drive". "Well don't think about it so much. Your sex drive is all in your head". "That`s what I mean. Ah want yer to lower it a bit".

The Honorary Secretary and Treasurer of the Wombwell Birth and Burial Benefit Society is owd Enoch Dobson. Ee`s told many a tale o`t`burials to `is mates at t`Wombwell Labour Club, Ee `as `em killing thersels not laughing at t`comic ways as some fowk `as died.

Like t`time Enoch went round for Joe`s subscription. Instead o`getting t`money ee finds Mrs. Joe now a widow and waiting to collect t`benefit. "Ee ah`m sorry to `ear Joe`s passed on," Enoch sez, putting `is collection book away.

"Can ah `ave a last look at `im? Ah`ve known `im since we war lads tha knows."

"Come in," sez Widow Joe. There int` parlour. Joe`s laid out, ready for t`undertaker.

"Well ah`ll be beggered," sez Enoch, "Ee does look well dunt ee".

"An` so ee should," sez Widow Joe, "we`d just come back from us `olidays i`Brid."

Enoch`s tactful an` ee knows ow to break bad news. Once when someone `ad drowned they`d sent t`bloke`s mate round to break t`news. Ee`d just gone up t`t` door, knocked and when t`Mrs. came eed said, "Are you t`widow Walker?"

"Ah`m nowt o`t`sort," she said, "ah`m married to Jack Walker".

"Tha`s not" t`mate replied, "that`s t`widow Walker. Ees drowned".

Enoch went round to Stubleys oo war months behind wi`t`dues. Ee knocks ont` door. Lilian Stubley comes to t`door wiping `er `ands on `er apron.

"Afternoon Mrs.," sez Enoch, "ahv`e come for t`dues. Bert in?"

"Nay, ee`s just killed hissen. Ee went down t`allotments to cut a cabbage an` ee`d `ad a few jars. Ee tripped ower t`marrow, fell ont`knife and killed hissen. Just like that".

"Ee ah`m reet sorry to hear that Mrs, " sez Enoch, who knows what`s to be done in these cases. "What did yer do?"

"Only thing we could do. We `ad to open a tin o`peas".

Enoch does it better. Ee knows we`ve all got to pop us clogs sometimes an` when ee tells `em t`widows don`t feel so bad about it.

So ee goes t`t`ouse, knocks on t`door, and breaks t`news tactful like.

"Ah`m reet sorry to `ave to tell yer, Mrs., but yer husband`s drowned to deearth i`t`beer vat at Barnsley Brewery".

"Ee that`s orful," she sez, "Cans`t tell me one thing. Did ee suffer much?"

"Nay, ah doant reckon so," Enoch sez, "they tell me ee `ad to get out three times to go t`t`lav."

One of t' sports reporters for t`Yorkshire Sports wor telling me as we did our arm bending exercises int`Alex t`other neet that Halifax Town`s manager rang up Don Revie (R.I.P.) at Leeds United for a spot of advice on how to get Halifax Town int` t`First Division like grown up clubs. T`telephone call went summat like this :-

Don Revie: "Allo".

Halifax Acting Manager, Captain, Groundsman and Bottle Washer: "`Alifax Town `ere Don. Can yer give us some `ints about `ow your lads train to get so good?"

Don Revie: "Happy to help lad. We need some competition. We lay out eleven dustbins in a team formation and each player dribbles the ball round them and tries to dazzle them with science. It improves ball control no end."

H.A.M.C.G.A.B.W.: "Thanks a million Don. We`ll try it. Remember me to Football".

Nice bloke Don, so a couple o` days later ees back ont`phone to `Alifax, anxious to find out how they`d got on.

Don Revie: "Allo, Leeds United `ere"

H.A.M.C.G.A.B.W.: "Allo Dave. `Alifax Town `ere".

Don Revie: "Well how did you get on with my new method of training?"

H.A.M.C.G.A.B.W.: "Bloody awful. T`dustbins won 2-1".

"T'dustbins won 2-1."

At a Yorkshire match agin Lancashire at Headingley there war this bloke there sticking his fillings in an` keepin` up a running commentary on t`match like :-

"What`s tha think that`s batting wi – a closet seat?"

"Weer`s tha white stick umpire?"

"My brother`s got more life in `im an` ees on t`sick"

"Kill t`umpire". "Kill t`batsman." "Kill t`bowler".

Ee war for killing that many folk there war some as thowt ee were an undertaker fra` Otley on a slack week. It went on for so long they `ad to send a committee member down fra`t`pavilion to `ave a word wi`im.

"Are you fra' Yorksher," sez t`committee member. "Nay," said t`bloke.

"Well, are yer fra` Lancashire". "Nay," sez t`bloke, wi` t`mouth like a parish oven.

"Well then," sez t`committee man, "tha mun mind thi own bloody business. Shut up." ee explained.

Yorkshire definition of optimism: Southern batsmen putting zinc on their noses.

"Ahm sorry to `ear tha` wife`s dead". "Not `alf as sorry as I am. I`d bought £40 of special pills to `elp `er get better an` she`d nobbit tekken two".

For a Sheffield lad, Eastern promise is a blind date in Doncaster.

Yorkshire fowk aren`t really rude. We just see fowk for what they are an` if they don`t like it it`s not our fault. There war this farmer out at Kilnsey. Small farm an only t`father an` son to run it. So there`s not much to talk about. Father`s dipping `is sheep when t`neighbour`s Land Rover roars int`t`yard an` out gets Farmer Harris, red faced with anger, shouting, "Do you know what that lad o` thine `as gone an` done now? Ee`s made our Mary pregnant. That`s what ee`s done. Ah`ll have `is guts for garters when I get me `ands on `im".

"Eee ee`s a dozy begger" sez t`father. "Ee went an` broke a shovel last week".

Down South tha can live next to fowk for years and nivver speak to `em. Not that they`d `ave owt worth saying if yer did. They may `ave all t`brass these days but they`re best ignored. Like the two Wharfedale farmers gone down to London during t`war to get away from t`urley of Burley. As they were strolling down Regent Street, gawping like hob-gobs, air-raid sirens went and everyone ran for shelters and tube stations. Except our two Tykes. A.R.P. man came hurtling up to them on a bike shouting, "Take cover. Take cover", but farmer Coverdale tells `im "Geronwiyer. It dunt apply to us. We doant live i`London".

"Mam, mam, t`milkman`s `ere. Ee says `ave yer got t`brass or should ah go out and play for a bit?"

Mi cousin Stan lives up i`Heptonstall. Ee went ower to Old Trafford for a Yorkshire versus Lancashire match last year an` ee`s sitting there an suddenly realises summat. "Damn it," ee sez in a loud voice. "Ah`ve left mi jock l`Ebden Bridge".

Silence all round while fowk tries to translate what he`s just said. "Never mind lad" says a kindly Lancastrian. "My wife`ll give you some lunch if you pop home during the break" (speaking slowly like they do when talking to someone who`s ten-pence to `t shilling). "Just go through yon gate, turn left around the back then turn right and there`s No. 23 Red Rose Row. My wife`ll cook lunch for you".

Stan`ll never refuse owt free. So off he trots. Two hours later ee`s back, brussen but flumoxed " Ah've got some reet bad news for thee. While I wor int' bedroom wi thi' wife after we'd etten us dinner t'chip pan caught fire an thi 'ouse burned down. Thi' wife's i' ospital." " Ee," said 'is Lanky pal wi' that phlegmatism born of a county weer life in't worth living, "Ah've got worse news for thee, Boycott's out".

The rooky police constable out on the beat finds a body floating in the canal at Brighouse. Bravely he leaps in, drags it half out, and begins desperately to give it artificial respiration just as he`s been taught in training school. Pressure. Spout of water. Pressure. Spout of water. Pressure. Spout...and so on. After twenty minutes calmly watching all this effort, owd George, stood behind him on t`canal bank, offers his advice. "Tha mun tek `is arse out o`t`watter, lad. Tha`s draining t`canal".

"They've tekken all t'sods off thi."

Taking a short cut through t'graveyard, Jack fell into a newly dug grave. "`Elp. `Elp! Ahm that cold ahm fair clammed. Ahm`cawd. Ahm`cawd". Ee bawls at t' top of his voice. Passing drunk hears the yelling, staggers over and and announces from t' grave edge "It`s no bloody wonder tha`s cawd lad. They`ve tekken all t`sods off thi".

Fred Trueman war bowling agin Lancashire wi`an umpire at came fra Rochdale an`   oo' war determined Lancashire war going to win – nay that`s impossible – ah mun mean not lose too badly. Fred bowls. Wham an` it `its `is pad stuck right in front o`t middle stump. "Owzat", yells Fred, an` `alf the team wi` `im. "Not out," says t`umpire. Next ball from Fred comes down. Wham. It `its t`bat and just whizzes past bail. T`bail shakes but dunt fall off. "Owzat," yells Fred. "Not out," says t`umpire, a bit annoyed like. Fred teks `is run again. Whizz. Wham. Crash, an` t`middle stump goes flying, sails twenty yards in t`air and crashes down, shattered. "By `ell," says Fred, "ah nearly `ad `im then".

Fred war in a Gentlemen versus Players game one time when they`d dredged round and got some real gentlemen. One o` `em came out to face Fred`s bowling. Strides out to the crease in leisurely fashion. Surveys the field slowly as if smelling each fielder. Teks ten minutes getting `is centre. Gets t`sight screen shifted, then adjusts `is gloves. "Ready now" ee finally calls.

Fred came pounding down and crack. Ee`s bowled first ball.

"Very good ball my man, " t`batsman calls to Fred on `is way back t`t`pavilion. Fred spits on `is `ands. "Aye but it war wasted on thee".

Enoch`s 85th birthday and his night of the year on a promise from 83 year old Edith that she`ll "see im reet ter neet". As she lies in bed waiting for the great moment, Enoch makes no move. No advances. Nothing. "Wot`s up wi`thi ter neet lad?" "Ee. Ah just can`t bring anybody ter mind.

"Wot's up wi' thi ter neet lad?"

A Leed's supporter from Unslet arrived at Elland Road that drunk 'ee passed out an' slept through t' game. Groundsmen found 'im afterwards and shook 'im awake with a friendly "Gerrome".

"Wot were t' score," t' lad asks,

"It war a draw- nil-nil"

"Oh aye, Well wot were t'score at 'alf time?"

Gargrave Hunt supporters go down to London to join a mass lobby. As one supporter watches the crowds surging into Parliament Square a policeman remarks "Crowded isn`t it?" "Ay, lad. There`s a coach load on us fra' Gargrave".

Little lad at Bradford City howling `is `ead off. "Ah`ve lost mi` dad". "What`s he like lad?" says t' policeman". "Tetley`s."

Owd Jack war playing Knurr an` Spell in`t field by t` Spring Rock i`Greetland when a funeral cortege led by a horse driven hearse went slowly down t`ill to Elland. Jack stopped `is game, took off `is flat `at and stood quietly as the procession passed. "That`s a reet nice gesture, Jack" said `is mate. "Ah didn`t know that tha` `ad that much respect fer t` dead". "Nay, we`ve been married 45 year. Ah owes `er summat".

In the clubs of South Yorkshire the lads are impossible to please. At t`Royston Working Men`s after being unable to make 'imself 'eard ower t' shouts of "Pies 'av cum" t`comic told t`Con. Sec., "I`m not going t'stage again unless I get a bit more attention". "Ah understand `ow tha feels" sez t`Con Sec. "Gerrout".

The new lad's act was a disaster. Mike Howl. Audience chunter. No-one heard a thing. No applause, just a few shouts of "Gerroff". The Con. Sec. Paid him off with a few words of sympathy "Don`t worry thissen lad. As ter thought o' gerrin' a job down t' pit?"

A nervous young singer read this inscription on the back of the door of his dressing room at Fryston Miners` Welfare:

Remember all ye who sit here before venturing forth to entertain the patrons of this club

Jesus Christ the one and only Son of God was booked in here for a week one Easter.

He did this truly amazing act of being crucified by sundry selected members of the audience, was certified dead by the Con. Sec. And was buried in the cellar under a barrel of mild.

Three minutes later he rose again and was back on stage.

Then there was the music teacher from Castleford who called his dog Grieg. "Because ee`s allus wantin` to pee a`gint suite".

Some fowk reckon we`re a bit rude in Yorkshire. A good thump on`t lug`ole`ll soon teach em better. We speak as we find. If we don`t like what we find then you can hardly blame us for pointing it out. Someone has to do it. Like mi mate Joss frae Thurgoland. Ee went down to London an` spent `is time for practically nowt going round an` round in t`underground ont`circle line. Joss war t`only bloke int` carriage when an ugly Southerner got on. Not just ugly. This bloke were like t`back end of a tram smash an` then some. Joss sat and stared at `im. Summat they don`t seem to do int`south. Eventually t`Southerner siz, "Just what are you staring at my good man?"

"Ah`m just thinking that tha`s t`ugliest begger ah`ve ever seen".

Poor Southern lad, "Well I can`t help it, can I?"

"No," sez Joss, "but tha could `ave stayed at `ome".

Joss war nowt if not direct. Ah mind t`time ee went into Penistone to catch t`bus to Barnsley for t`market. It`s Joss`s turn to get on when t`conductor puts his arm across an` pushes Joss off again. "Gerroff," sez t`conductor, "we`re full. Tha`ll `ave to wait for t`next".

"Oh aye," sez Joss, "an` `ow long`ll that be?"

Conductor thinks ee`s a right wit. "About thirty feet, like this un".

"Oh aye", sez Joss, "an` will it `ave a closet ont`back wi a turd in like this un?"

"I don't know how much he charges for oor Willie."

That seems to 'appen a lot int' Dales. Nowt else to do. A Bilsdale farmer facing exactly the same complaint dashed into 'is neighbour Farmer Blaydon`s farm to tell `im `is son had made `is lass pregnant. Blaydon`s wife came to the door. "Made her pregant `as ee" she said thoughtfully. "Well, you`ll have to wait til my husband comes home. I know ee charges ten bob for t' boar and £5 for t' stallion. But I don`t know how much ee charges for oor Willie".

The three wise men who brought Gold and Frankincense and Myrrh to the baby Jesus actually came from Yorkshire, the only place they could find that many wise men. This isn`t generally recognised but the Bible makes it quite clear. "Three wise men came from the East Riding on camels".

Fred from Heckmondwike sees `is mate with a big bag ower `is shoulder. "What`s tha got in yon bag?" "Chickens" "If ah guess `ow many tha`s got will ter gi us one?" "Aye. If tha guesses `ow many ah`ve got then tha can `ave `em both". "Reet" sez Fred "Nah then. Let`s see. Ow about five?"

Bert goes int' crowded pub looking worried "Does anyone `ere own a girt black cat wi a white collar?" No answer. "God `elp me. Ah`ve run ower t`vicar".

Ther`s this posh bloke at t' bar at t' Ring o'Bells and my mate`s Yorkie walks straight up to him and cocks his leg up against `is Ush Puppies. Bloke didn`t say a word. In fact ee war that nice about it ee took three crisps out of `is bag and threw `em on`t floor for t`dog. Mi mate war dead relieved. "That`s very nice of you" he sez, "t`dog wets thi trousers and tha gives `im a crisp".

"Aye" said the bloke, "an` when I see which end picks t`crisp up I`ll stick me boot int`t`other".

But then they are a bit taciturn like that in the Dales. In Pateley Bridge there were two farm hands stood in t'road just outside ` vicarage, fratching bitterly about what looked to me to be a dead horse. "It`s a donkey". "Is it eck it`s a mule". "Ah tell thi it`s a donkey". "Tha needs thi `ead looking at. It`s a mule".

So it went on until the Rev. Fawthrop was drawn out by the noise. Being a man of the cloth he quickly calmed them down. "It`s an ass. It`s the same animal that carried our Lord into Jerusalem. We must bury it with all due respect".

Reluctantly they agreed and began digging. Major Bagshaw appeared round the corner. Once a soldier always a soldier. He called out, "What`s that you`re digging men? A fox hole?"

"Not according t`t`Vicar".

Vicar going round his new parishioners in Hubberton. "Why do you have this bucket of manure in your lounge?" "Ter keep t`flies out o`t`kitchen yer daft bugger".

Leeds rag trade sweatshop posts a new notice in t'toilet. "Because we are working on pastels employees must always wash their hands on leaving the toilet". Indeed, the boss is so worried he questions his workers as they come out. "Did yer wash yer hands?" "Nay, we`re not going back t`workshop. We`re off to 'ave u's dinner."

Proud Jewish father in Alwoodley breaks the bad news to his wife. "We`ve got to face it. Us son`s an `omosexual." Loud sobbing. But he comforts her. "It could be worse. He`s in love with a doctor".

Ave yer `erd t`one about this poor upset lass from Sheffield oo didn`t even know she`d been raped until t`cheque bounced?

Nellie, up in the heights of Mount Tabor, falls ill and can`t get out. Asks her miserable old neighbour who walks into Halifax most days if he`ll call in t`Post Office and see if there`s a packet there for her. Grudgingly he goes off and equally grudgingly calls back in t` evening. "Aye. It`s theer alreet".

What's the difference between a Lancastrian and a computer? You only have to punch information into a computer once.

"Doctor. Ah'v got a girt pain i` mi left arm." "Don`t worry. It`s nobbut awd age". "But ah`v nowt in t`reet arm and ah'v ad it just as long.

Two Hull lads met in the Earl De Gray (R.I.P.).

One had a brown dog the other a black and they argued who`s was the fiiercest. The dogs flexed their muscles, growled and bared their teeth.

"My dog could murder yours" said the brown dog`s master.

"My dog could crucify yours" said the black dog`s master.

"Oh shut up will yer" said the landlord. "Ah`ve got a dog behind here will lick both those things at t`same time".

The match was agreed. One gave his dog a whisky, the other slipped his a sherry with an egg whisked up in it. Then the landlord produced his dog. Spotted with very short legs.

Slowly it lurched over to the brown dog and ate it. Then it did the same with the black dog.

As it belched the dog owners sobbed,

"Ere, what kind o`dog is that?"

"Well" replied the landlord, "afore I lopped its tail off an painted t`spots on it, it were a crocodile".

Owd Joss is due for `is 87th birthday in`t`Golden Autumn `ome i`Adwick le Street. So t`staff decides to commemorate the great day by hiring a Doncaster prostitute as a strip o`gram girl. Owd Joss is getting ready for t`party when in she comes. Stark naked.she announces loudly "Ah`m bahn ter gi' thi Super Sex". Joss stares resignedly. "If it`s all t`same ter thee love, ah`ll just ave t`soup".

Visitor to the Dales. "Where, my man, does virgin wool come from?" "Ee tha daft bugger. It comes from t`sheep we can`t catch".

There`s lads i`Barnsley that religious they won`t work if there`s a Sunday in`t week.

A Labour Party meeting in true blue Selby:
Candidate: "If you good people vote for us we will bring down Income Tax."
Voice from back: "What about t`Owd Age Pensions?"
Candidate: "If you good people vote for us we will increase Old Age Pensions."
Voice from back: "What about t`prostitutes on our streets?"
Candidate: "If you good people vote for us we will drive prostitution underground."
Voice from back: "Bloody Labour. Pampering t`miners again."

An American taking a Leeds taxi out to Elmet boasts about how fast they build in the States. "We built the Empire State Building in just 36 months". At that moment they pass the huge Social Security building at Quarry Hill. "Say, what`s that, buddy?" "Dunno. It wern`t `eer this morning".

"Bloody Labour. Pampering t'miners again!"

Relations with Lancashire have never been good because Yorkshire's all hills an moors, Lancashire's all mills an`...well perhaps not all. There's always been a lot o`fratching which began wi`t`Wars ot`Roses. Red rose versus white. T`white rose won of course an` General Trumpington-Blatherskite's Short History of Yorkshire Victories (14 volumes) tells us that t`Earl of Derby was marching ower t`Pennines wi a huge Lancashire army. They spot a Yorkshireman on Studley Pike shouting "One Yorkshireman can beat fifty on yer". So to make sure they send 100 Lancashire soldiers after him. None came back.

Next day there he was shouting "One Yorkshireman can beat 100 on yer".

This time they send 200.

This went on for three days until one battered, bloodstained, Lancashire sodjer staggered back into the Red Rose camp. "Let's get back home" ee gasped. "It's a trap. There's two of `em".

Lad applying for newspaper delivery job under EU rules on Child Labour is asked by t' gaffer "Aren`t thee t`lad as come last week an` I said ah wanted an older lad?"

"Aye, that`s reet. But this week ahm older".

A little lad `is just grabbing summat int`pantry when 'is mother grabs `im. "Ow is it I allus catches thi stealin t`jam?" "It`s them soft slippers".

"It's a trap. There's two of 'em."

A Huddersfield wife goes into the bank to cash her husband's cheque. The teller refuses, telling her it needs endorsing. She takes it away and comes back shortly with "Your loving wife Ethel" written across it.

Gallup Poll in Ollerton asks people what they think of sex on the television. 95% said "Reet uncomfortable".

A Whitby nun died exhausted after being repeatedly raped by Viking raiding parties. Finding herself in Viking Valhalla she's horrified to find that the god in charge makes a pass at her. "You cannot reject me. I'm Thor". "Oh yes I can – how do you think I feel".

Little lads paddling at Scarborough. "Ee tha feet's mucky". "Aye, we didn't come last year".

It was two in the morning and a lamp flickered in an upstairs window of the tiny farm in Rosedale.

For Bill and Babs Bugby it was a great moment. Bill was holding the lamp as Doctor Foster was preparing to deliver his first-born.

Suddenly the Doctor held up a baby boy. Bill leaned nearer with the lamp to have a look.

"Ho'd on" said the Doctor, "there's another one cummin'." Then he held up a baby girl.

"Twins" gasped Bill as he held the lamp nearer to have a look.

"Ho'd on" cried the Doctor, as out popped another baby boy.

Suddenly the room was pitched into darkness and Bill's boots clattered off down the stairs.

"Bring back that lamp" yelled the Doctor.

"No fear" shouted back Bill from the parlour. "Tha'll 'ave to manage baht it – t'dammed leet's attractin' t'little beggars".

"Leave Grim alone. Ee's t'Boss."

As yet another Viking raiding party lands in Grimsby. Grim theer leader announces "We`re going to rape all the men and rob all the women". His deputy tugs his sleeve, "You`ve got that wrong way round". From the back of the crowd comes a loud lisping voice, "Leave Grim alone. Ee`s t`boss."

49

Scratch even the poshest Harrogate type Yorkshireman and you`ll find pure Tyke close to the surface. Take Joe Clogroyd, a miner at Waterloo Main `oo struck lucky on t`pools an` copped £100,000.

Leaves `is back to back. Sells `is whippet. Ups to live i`Gargrave. Ee joins t`hunt.

Ee cut a marvellous figure on `is new `orse `ad a great chase an` was in on the death. Next day the Hunt Master comes round to Joe`s new palace. "Look Mister Clogroyd" sez ee, "this is rather embarrassing and I don`t want you to take it at all personal. But it is customary for riders to hounds to call `Tally Ho` rather than `Kill t`bushy tailed bastard."

Asked for his daughter`s hand in matrimony t`owd Dales farmer says "Would tha still love `er if she`d no brass?" "Oh yes. I love her so much". "then tha`d better tek thi `ook lad. Ah`v enough foils in`t family already".

A Dalesman on his first visit to Leeds was stopped by the police for driving his old banger the wrong way up a one-way street. "And where do you think you`re going?" "Er, ahm non too sure. But ah mun` be late. They`re all cummin back".

A tonic for t'wife.

A North Yorkshire farmer goes t`t`doctor. "Ah need summit for t`wife. Yesterday she got up at four, milked t`cows, got us breakfast, then went out and ploughed t`top field, fed t`chickens, repaired t`roof and then said she wor too tired to do owt else. Can tha gi` us a tonic for `er?"

Then there were the two old Dalesmen who lived in two old dilapidated cottages in Wensleydale. They were leaning on the garden wall talking to each other.

"Nar then Joe, ah'v just `ad a letter from t'council, They`re moving me into a new council flat next week".

"That`s great" his friend says "but what are you going to do with your pig?"

"Well I`m taking him with me" he replied.

"But where are you going to put him?" Joe asks.

"I`m going to put him in the bedroom!"

"But what about the smell?" Joe asks

"Chuff t`smell, pig`ll soon get used to it".

After spending weeks fattening up his pigs Fred Pickles drove them all down to Pickering market to sell them off.

In the pub he met `is owd mate, Tom, who fancied buying a few pigs. Fred wanted a quick sale and a bargain was struck. Fred let Tom have the pigs at a very reasonable price.

"Ah`ll send thi a cheque in t`post" said Tom. They had a few bevvies to seal the deal.

Well two weeks later Fred still hadn`t hear a dickybird from Tom. So he sent him a letter saying he`d appreciate the money.

He got one back saying "next week". This went on for months until the two met again in the pub on market day.

"Bah lad" muttered Fred, "Ahm reet feet up wi' thee. If ah`d ha` known tha was nivver goin` ti pay, ah`d ha`charged thi twice as much".

Little lad twagging school rings up t`teacher. "Johny won`t be coming to school terday. This is his feyther".

Lad from Mixenden goes into t`butcher and orders a steak. "Is it tender?" "Tender?" says the butcher "Why it`s as tender as your wife`s `eart". "Then gi` us some chops".

Fred gets on the Manchester train at Halifax and starts chatting to his neighbour who`s not at all responsive. So to lighten the atmosphere he decides to tell a few jokes. "Ah`ll tell thi a joke about two Lancashire hob gobs in a balloon and….." "I think you should know I`m a Lancastrian myself". "That`s alreet. Ah`ll tell it reet slow".

There`s no mines left in Barnsley but a hell of a lot of miners on t`New Lodge Estate. One on`em, Jack Obbs, went down to London to see life an' booked in t`to t`Park Lane `Ilton. When they ask `im ter sign t`register ee makes `is cross. Just then there`s a gorgeous blonde walks past an` Jack sez t`t`page "Bloody Ummer, I could do wi a bit o`that." Page sez "Well I think it might be possible to arrange a rendezvous for Sir, on the side you understand".

"Well gerron wi`it then" sez Jack, grabbing hold of t`register an`putting a ring round `is cross.

"Pardon me, but why has Sir just done that".

"Tha dunt think as ah`m goin` ter go traipsing around wi` yon blonde bit under mi own name does tha?"

A Texan visiting Yorkshire had been told that we`re the Texas of Britain; the biggest and the best. A lone star state with the same "Think Big" tradition. Up in the Dales he`s disappointed by the tiny farms. "Do you know" he says to a Dales farmer ower t`wall, "My farm`s so big it takes me four days to drive from end to end of it". "Aye, ah know how tha` feels. I used to `ave a car like that".

Owd Ezra fra Dent wor persuaded at 72 to buy `is first Lottery ticket. In fact ee got that excited ee bought two. Sunday it wor announced as ow` eed won £8 million quid. So t`reporter, editor and printer (all t`same bloke) went from t`Dent Dalesman to do t`interview. "Ow dos`t a feel, Ezra? It mun bi marvellous to win all that brass". "Marvellous be buggered. Ah`m reet peeved. T`other ticket won nowt"

Jez Fannackapan fra Malham wor that fed up when all `is lambs wor killed cos o't' Foot and Mouth ee decided to commit suicide. So ee went to t`nearest chemist i`Gargrave. "Gie us twenty pence worth of arsenic, ahm bahn to kill missen". Dead worried, the assistant rings the Samaritans. "I`ve got Jez Fannackapan in`t pharmacy. Ee wants twenty pence worth of arsenic to kill issen. Whot shall I do?" "Tell im t`smallest quantity you do costs two pund. That`ll stop im."

There's these two old birds sitting int' Priestley Bingo i`Bratford named after t`best caller Bratford ever `ad. There's a funeral procession goes past outside. When she sees it thru` t`winder one old bird begins to snuffle and sniffle that much she misses two calls. "What's up wi`thi" says t`other. "Eee" she sez "ah`m upset. Ee wor a good husband to me".

Yorkshireman and his lad on holiday at Squires Holiday Camp, Blackpool. No brass but they're desperate to have a flight from the airport there and whitter on and on at the pilot. "We`ve ony got 50p but we mun fly. Will t`a tek us?" Pilot refuses but they worrit on more. He gets thoroughly fed up by this incessant whittering so on the last day, when they`re only still offering only 50p to fly them he finally agrees. "All right. I`ll take you. In fact, if you stop whittering I`ll give you the 50p back." The plane goes off on a marvellous Round Tour and flies upside down, round the Tower, loops the loop and gives them the best tour they could have, all of it received in total silence. On landing the pilot reluctantly coughs up "Here's your 50p back. At least you stayed shut up for the whole flight." "Aye" says the Yorkshireman. "But ah nearly ad to say summat when t`lad fell out".

Harrogate. The place where people spend money they haven`t got, to buy things they don`t need, to impress folk they don`t like.

"Tha' knows that tha telt mi that car tha selt us `ad only been owned by one little old lady?" "Look" said the Leeds super salesman, "it doesn`t come with any guarantees. So don`t think you can complain to Trading Standards". "Nay, it`s not that. She left a packet o`Durex and five copies of "Big and Busty" in`t glove box and she might want `em back".

Colonel Bagshaw-Smyth from Knottingley Manor House went out to Pakistan to advise the Pakistani Post Office an` found `em all very `ard working and conscientious. Until he got to a big town in the interior. There everyone was lying around, sunbathing, eating ice cream an` doing nowt at all. "What the devil`s going on here? Why are you all lazing around?" he bawls in best military fashion. "Well, Sahib", the postmaster explains. "This is Bowling Tide week".

Undertekker calls on owd Seth, oo`s 93, to drum up a bit o` business. "If tha meks a desposit now on thi funeral, tha`ll get it cheaper. "Nay, ah`ll not bother. Ah could be drowned at sea.

Bus to Bradford from `Uddersfield comes in after `Uddersfield Town `ad been lossin` at `ome. The bus is packed. "Sorry" bawls the Pakistani conductor. "Me ram-jam full". Bloke at the front o`n t`queue bawls out, "Ah don`t want to know thi name. Ah just want to get ont`bloody bus".

Reet after t`war when folk fra South Yorksha went for their `olidays ter t`Costa del Caravan i`Cleethorpes and Bradford went ter Morecambe, young Jack fra Bentley Colliery won t`Co-op prize for an `oliday i`foreign parts i`Italy. A week i`Venice bi t`Grand Canal, wi no fishing an no dead dogs floating, unlike t`canals ee knows. First neet int`otel Jack puts is flat `at an kerchief on and goes down to dinner. "Will you ava de soup, sir". "Nay. Ah`ll just ave fish an chips." "You must ava de soup. Is delicious Ministrone, speciality of Italy". "Nay". "I`ll fetch da manager to tell you about the soup". Manager comes. "Sir must avva de soup. Is delicious Ministrone." "Nay, ah don`t want soup." "Is speciality of Italy. We very proud of our soup". "Ah don`t give a bugger. Ah just want fish and chips like i`Bentley". More muttered argument about "da soup" but eventually, and reluctantly, the fish and chips finally come.

Joe eats and goes off to bed to dream of home. At 3.30am the reception desk gets a call from Room 353, a hotel visitor with violent stomach pains and constipation. They send the doctor up with an enema but mistakenly he`s given the number of Room 535 where Joe lies blissfully asleep, counting coll tallies. Reluctant to wake him the doctor administers the enema and goes quietly out. At the end of the week after carefully comparing Venice with the delights of Doncaster, Joe goes back to Bentley. There he`s eagerly asked by the Co-op travel department to recommend Italy so they can attract more customers. "Well, Venice is all reet but ah`ll give tha one bit of advice. When they ask you to `ave t` soup tek it. If yer don` they`ll come and shove it up thi arse in t`middle of t`neet."

Overheard in Heppy's Fish Restaurant in Wakefield:

"Ah wor reet sorry ah couldn't get to Bob's Bachelor Party last week. Wor it a good do?"

"Wor it eck. Everyone theer wor able to go to work t'next day".

At Yorkshire primary schools t'Band of Ope used to go round tellin t' kids about t' evils of alcohol. T' ighlight o't lecture wor when they'd put a wriggly worm in't alcohol an' it 'ud die. Dead quick. At Woodbottom Council School t'Band Major then asked t' kids "So wot dusta learn from that?" Smelly Walker put 'is 'and up. "Please Sir. If tha's got worms tha'd better drink alcohol".

"Well, that operation was just in the nick of time" said the Dore surgeon in his private hospital. "You mean the patient was about to die?" "No. He'd have recovered by himself in a few hours' time".

Owd Seth, t'meanest bugger i'Skipton, rings t'Craven Herald to put 'is wife's death notice in t' paper. To save money he makes it simple. "Leah Greenwood's dead". The telephonist says "There's a minimum charge of £5 for thirty words. Don't you want to add something more to use the space?" "Well tha' can put 'second 'and wheel chair for sale. One owner. Not much used."'

Chap took a pub in a tiny village near Grassington. As soon as he opened the doors in staggered an old yokel not a day under eighty. He glowered at t`landlord, spat on t`fire, hobbled to a seat in t' corner and began bashing t`floor wi `is stick.

"What`s tha want?" sez t`new landlord.

"Look" said t' owd lad."Mi name`s Ned. Ah`m t`owdest in t`village and when I come in I allus sit `ere. And when I bangs me stick I want a gill o`mixed reet sharp. So think on."

Gritting his teeth the landlord served him. An` in walks the squire.

"Good Day my man" said the squire. "I`ll have six bottles of gin, eight bottles of Scotch, a dozen of sherry and a dozen of port. Oh, yes, and six crates of Tetley`s Pale Ale and six of Guinness. Get your cellarman to put them in my Landrover. And won`t you join me in a large Scotch!"

As the squire and the new landlord supped up, old Ned war banging like fury wi` `is stick. Turning beetroot wi` anger t`landlord pulls a half to slam down before old Ned but as he approaches old Ned looks up: "Look lad. I`ll gi thi a bit of advice. Thee look after thi regulars. Yon buggar only comes in once a week".

Arthur an`Ted are sitting `aving a quiet pint in`Victory Club I`Stocksbridge. They`ve just read t`Sun so they`re talking about t' Permissive Society an` `ow much it cost to join. "Yer know old mate" sez Arthur "ah nivver `ad any sexual relations wi`t`wife before ah married `er....Did thee?" "Dunno" sez Ted "wot war `er maiden name?"

Yorkshireman arrives at the gates of heaven. "Where are you from?", asks St. Peter. "Yorkshire" says the lad proudly. "Then bugger off. We're not cooking Yorkshire Pud for one!"

In Heckmondwike there's not much to do except watch t'grass grow, so they live to a ripe old age. But none older than Josiah Igginbotham, t'owdest inhabitant at 95. T'Round Table got together an proposed that they should do summat special to commemorate Josiah's 95th birthday. Ee'd nivver been out of Heckmondwike in 'is life so they decided to club together and send 'im to London. New suit, new suitcase, new 'aircut an' off ee went. Two days later ee war back. Unimpressed. "Wot war it like?" they asked.

"Well, ah'll tell thi this. Heckmondwike 's better ner London".

Ee war so contented that ee reached 105. This time t'Round Tablers as an even bigger whip round t'table an' sent 'im to Paris for a week. Same thing 'appened:

"Heckmondwike's better ner Paris" ee declared.

They didn't need to spend any more money sending 'im ter Sheffield for t'day. Ee died at 109 an' passed ower to t' other side. An' this time ee 'ad to admit it. 'Is eyes opened wide. 'Is mind marvelled. Soon ee couldn't contain 'is wonder. "Ah've got ti admit it" ee yelled. "'Eaven's better na Heckmondwike". Just then up came a man wi' a long tail and a pitchfork an' sez "Shut up you old fool. This isn't heaven".

"'Eaven's better na Heckmondwike."

Yorksher`s a language all on its own. When t`Yorkshiremen on t`test team (that used to bi nearly all o`t`team) didn`t want to be overheard all they `ad to do war to talk i`Yorksher. So there`s a lot o` jokes no one from South o`Doncaster can understand. Like the bloke from Oxford who was asking the class at St. Helen`s County Primary in Monk Bretton where they were going for their holidays. Course they all were going to Bridlington. Except one lad oo pipes up, "Mi dad`s tekkin` us t`t`lakes i`Barnsley". "Then he`s pulling your leg sonny, there`s no lakes in Barnsley.". Little lad dunt agree, "Well mi dad sez there`s more lakes na works i`Barnsley".

Denise, a French au-pair girl, wer dead miserable I' Hull. There`s nowt to do after 8 o`clock an` it`s I`only place ah`ve ever been where t`taxi drivers ask you where they can get a woman.

So Denise is crying `er eyes out one night in`t Wellington Club when she bumps into a sailor oo sez ee`ll take `er back `ome to France. Provided she`ll sleep in `is cabin with `im. She agrees an` ee smuggles `er on board that very night.

T`ship sails next morning. It`s dead rough and t`sailor`s no gentleman but a reet Yorkshireman oo wants value for t`money ee`s not spent. Five days later after `is insatiable sexual demands night and day she thinks they must now be in France. Sea sick, battered, bedraggled she staggers on t`bridge t`t`captain and sez "Oooo Monsieur, I am sorry, I am ze stowaway. Please. We must be in France by now".

"France lass?" sez the Captain, "France? This is t`Hull to Grimsby Ferry".

"We'll only have sheep droppings to eat..."

After the worst Viking raid in years the Abbot of Whitby Abbey calls the remaining monks together. "First the bad news. The Vikings have raped all the nuns, made off with our food stores for the winter, and taken all the gold. So we'll only have sheep droppings to eat this winter". "What's the good news?" "There's plenty of sheep out there on them moors".

The Eastbrook Hall in Bradford was the scene of Yorkshire's best `ell fire preaching. Every week Rev. Shuttlebotham would preach against demon drink, fornication, gambling and covetousness. As the sermon rose to its rousing crecendo with Rev. Shuttlebotham invoking the threat of hell fire for all the fornicators, drinkers and gamblers in Bradford some in the congregation, terrified of the fate awaiting them, cried out "Forgive us Lord. Forgive us. We didn`t know what we were doing". At which Rev. Shuttlebotham shouted back "Well, tha` knows now! Tha knows now!"

Even outside London it`s sometimes difficult for decent Yorkshire fowk to get therselves understood. Jack Higgins took a week off from Kellingley to go to Wales. Couldn`t understand a word they said until after four days he found someone to teach him Welsh. He recited his Welsh phrases over an` over in bed. Next morning up early to try them out. Not a soul around. Even in the country round about; not a soul. Ee`s about to give up an` go back to bed. Then ee sees a lonely figure on a bike pedalling towards him. As the figure drew nearer Jack leapt into the road shouting: "Jacky Da. Jacky Da". The cyclist kicked `im out of the road an` grunted, "Get out o`t`road yer dozy Welsh bastard".

"Dad. Dad. Ahv just saved 20p running `ome behind t` school bus. "Tha daft bugger" says dad. "Why didn`t tha run `ome behind a taxi and save £5?"

Some Yorkshire fowk are that mean they wudn`t tell yer tomorrow war Tuesday if yer didn`t ask `em. They wouldn`t part wi`t`reek o` their own muck. Most`on us aren`t that mean but we do chuck us money around like a man wi`no arms. Ow do yer think millowners get to be millowners if it in`t by waiting to read t`Telegraph an` Argus until it`s wrapped round their fish an` chips? T`meanest on `em war Percy Craddock, a reet self-made man oo worshipped `is creator.

When ee retired from t`business ee decides to part wi` some o` t`brass an` sets off on a world cruise on a liner that big it made Saltaire Mills look like our pigeon loft. Ee`ad t`best suite on A deck. Air condimenting, two stewards.

First day on board t`Purser comes. "Captain`s compliments Mr. Craddock. He`s asked me to request the pleasure of the company of yourself and Mrs. Craddock at his table for the duration of the voyage." "Then ee must be daft" says Craddock. "After ah`ve paid all that good brass for t`tickets tha don`t expect me to eat wi`t`crew does tha?"

Still at least we`ve not as much to learn as they `ave in some parts. Ah mind the Todmorden tackler oo left t`town just before t`first World War wi Bill Holt. Bill went to Germany. `Is mate Tom went to Paris. Tom got back first. A tackler`s a prince among weavers an` when ee`d cum back they clustered round `im wi`awe. "Is it like they say it is i`Paris?" they said. "Well, ah can`t say much" ee sez wi`t`dignity tacklers `ave. "But ah`ll tell thi this. Sexual Intercourse is in its infancy i`Todmorden".

A Dales farmer's on the bus back home from Skipton. Sitting next to a chatty American tourist doing the Dales who chatters on trying to get the taciturn farmer talking:

"Say, did you have a good day at market today?"

"`Appen".

"I think Skipton's a beautiful place. Don`t you agree?"

"`Appen".

"This surely must be one of the most beautiful parts of Yorkshire".

"`Appen".

"What a beautiful dog. Have you had him long?"

"`Appen".

"And what`s the little fellow`s name?"

"Roger Bacon".

At last. A chink in the conversational armour. So she forged in. "What an unusual name for a dog. Why on earth do you call him Roger Bacon?"

"Because o`what ee does t` t`pigs".

In the Earl de Grey pub in Hull a bloke comes in with a tiny piano and a little pianist only a foot high. He sets both down on the bar and the pianist begins to play. Beautifully. After half a dozen numbers the amazed regulars takes a collection and hand it to the visitor. "That's amazing" says the landlord watching it all. "Where did you get him"? "Well ah found a bottle on t` beach at Spurn Point. Ah rubbed it and a genie came out. He gave me one wish and here I am wi`t bloody twelve inch pianist. T' bloody Genie wor deaf!"

Wetwang is not far from Driffield in what's renamed the East Riding. Sheila cum `ome back ter Wetwang full of ersen after t`first term at York University. First thing she sees is her dad wielding t`pitch-fork."Hello daddy" she says, as though she had a mouthful of broken glass, "do tell me what you are doing".

"Muck spreadin`," he grunts.

Young Sheila let fly at her mam.

"Really, mummy, I do think you ought to do something about father`s language. Can`t you ask him to say `manure-spreading`?"

"Nay, lass," said her mam. "It`s tekken me twenty year to git him to call t`bloody stuff muck".

Muck spreadin'.

Grandma from Harrogate went down to Barnsley to look after her daughter's kids while Jack and Jenny were on holiday. She was appalled by the kids' language. Next morning determined to ignore it she said to young Jack "Good morning sweetheart and what would you like for breakfast'. "Ah'll ave some of them bleeding cornflakes". She said "You mustn't speak like that". As a punishment just to teach him to speak properly "It's no cornflakes for you". She then belted him round the lugs and turned to the granddaughter to ask her "What would you like for breakfast, Sally?" "Well, ah'll noan `av` any of them bloody cornflakes".

Bloke goes round to see his friend. T`friend's wife answers the door. "Excuse me Missus, is Fred in?". "Nay" says she, "ee`s gone up t'mill to get cotton." "Oh" says t`bloke, "I'll call again tomorrow".

The next day ee`s back. "Ello Missus, is Fred in?" "Nay" says the wife, "he's gone up t'mill again to get cotton."

T`bloke leaves it a week an calls again. "is Fred in today?" "No" says the wife, "haven't you heard, he died last weekend. "Well ah`m reet sorry to 'ear that" sez the bloke, "Have you buried him yet?" Yes replied the wife, "he's buried in't graveyard at top o't hill." "Well," says t' bloke "I'd better go and pay 'im me last respects then".

Up the hill he goes searches for Fred's grave and reads on t`headstone, "Gone. But not for cotton".

Yorkshire fowk don`t let money go to their `eads – or to anyone else`s pockets. Like old Joss Akroyd i`Royston. Saturday neet ee finds out ee`s won £400,000 on t`pools. More money than Vivienne Nicholson`s spent. Ee celebrates all day Sunday but come Monday morning ee`s int`clocking in queue back at Redfearn`s. "Nay, Joss, that`s not going to carry on working nah that tha`s won 400,000 quid are yer?"

"Not I, me old love," sez Joss, "ah`ve cum back for me pot".

Still that`s not as mean as a lad ah was at school wi` at Woodbottom Council School. Ee`s living i`Baildon an` tekin out this lass from Riddlesden ten miles away. So they meet in Bingley but allus inside t`Myrtle cinema so ee dunt `ave to pay for `er.

When they come out ee let`s `er pay for `is fish and chips across in`t Myrtle Fish Bar. Ee won`t tek `er `ome cos it`ll cost too much to go there `an back on`t`bus so ee gives `er a tanner for `er fare.

Off she goes, tramps up `ome and bursts inter tears telling `er mother all about `ow mean ee`s been.

"`Ah nivver `eard nowt like it, the skinny devil. Ere`s a couple o' bob. Get t`bus and tek `im back `is tanner this minute". So she goes back on`t`bus all the way to Baildon and marches up to `is door i`Woodbottom.

"`Ello luv. Forgotten summat?" "Nay, me mam sez to give yer yer tanner back. An `ere it is" and wi that she chucks it at `im. "Nay" ee sez. "Tha shouldn`t`a bothered. It`d a` done int`morning".

Herbert was feeling lonely. So ee bought a lovely pup – a black Cocker Spaniel – little an` daft, wi big eyes like a baby.

"Tha`s a reet beauty" said Herbert, as the pup licked his face, "even tho` tha`s good for nowt".

He took t`pup for a walk by t' canal an` threw a stick in. Next thing he knows t`pup is after it, trotting across t' surface of the canal.

Back comes the pup with the stick and Hebert picks him up. Pup`s feet are bone dry.

Off he ran to his mate, Charley, and dragged him down to t`Canal bank.

"Nah then" says Herbert, "just thee watch this". Ee hurles t' stick across t' water. Off goes t`pup, toddles over t`water and comes back with t`stick – bone dry.

Charley just howls wi laughter.

"Ere" says Herbert, "ere cleverclogs, shut up laughin` and admit me pup`s a ruddy marvel. A reet bargain for a fiver".

"Bargain," spluttered Charley, "Bargain!. Tha`s been done `Erbert. Yon bloody mutt can`t even swim".

Why do Dales shepherds always marry Dales women? Sheep can't cook.

*Next thing he knows t'pup is trotting across
t'surface of t' canal.*

An ostrich wandering aimlessly round Knaresborough was lassooed by a visitor and taken to the police station. There the rookie constable was worried stiff. What should he do about the big bird? "Sergeant I don`t know what on earth to do wi` this `ere ostrich". "Use your imagination" came the impatient reply, "tek it t` bloody zoo".

Exit constable and bird. Hours later the sergeant was walking his beat when constable and bird loomed into view. "What the `ell are you doing wi` yon ostrich? Ah tel`t thi` to tek it t`t zoo". "Aye, a did but ee didn`t like that. Now we`re off t`t pictures."

Young Barry ran to scoil down t`snicket past Charlton`s Farm every morning, yelling as he ran :

"Hey Charlton. Oo puts watter in t`milk?"

After weeks of this Farmer Charlton gets reet sick on it and complains to Barry`s headteacher. Barry got a real ticking off and was told ee`d get t`cane if he shouted that again.

Next morning came the clatter of Barry`s clogs. Farmer Charlton looked up from milking and grinned. Then he heard Barry`s voice.

"Hey" shouted Barry.

"What`s up now?" demanded Charlton.

"Tha knows!" yelled Barry.

By now tha` should know what sort of man a Yorkshireman is. A reet`un. But there`s some rum uns too. Like t`bloke standing on top o't` Merrion Centre i`Leeds threatening to commit suicide. "Mi wife`s left me. I`m going to end it all" ee yells. A bloke from Heckmondwike uses good Yorkshire commonsense and shouts up t`bloke. "Don`t do a daft thing like that. Think about yer Yorkshire Pudding on Sunday".

"I`m going to jump".

T`Heckmondwike bloke decides to make `im laugh wi a Yorkshire joke about someone dying.

"I`m going to jump".

"Think about t`lovely county. Think ont`Dales. Think on Ilka Moor".

"I`m going to jump".

"Well think about our Freddy".

"Freddy? Freddy who?"

"Jump yer beggar. Jump".

"Ee my wife`s a dirty bugger. Useless at cleaning t`ouse". "Well it looks pretty clean to me". "Tha knows nowt. Ivvery time I go to pee in`t sink it`s full o` dirty dishes".

Has ter `eard t`one about t`Barnsley lad who picked his nose so deep he pulled t`lining of his flat `at down?"

A Barnsley couple had longed for children but weren`t blessed with any until both were in their forties when the wife gave birth to a fine strapping young lad. Their pride and joy was treated like a Royal baby. Which, of course, he was, growing up in Barnsley. As he grew older the lad was a perfectly normal kid just like all the others. He loved his food, especially his Yorkshire pud. Yet he never talked, or uttered so much as a word.

The couple got more and more worried. The lad reached three, four, five, without talking. Even when he started at school he never spoke despite all the efforts of the Educational Psychologist who could find nothing at all wrong with the lad. Except that he said nowt.

So it went on. Until, suddenly, one Sunday at Sunday dinner the lad pushed away his Yorkshire pud saying loudly "Yon Yorkshire pudden`s sad". The couple were as worried as they were delighted. "Ee lad, that`s said nowt all these years. What`s suddenly got thi talking about t`Yorkshire?"

"Well, there war nowt wrong wi' mi' Yorkshire pudden afore" sez t`lad.

Barnsley lad on parachute training is told to leap from the plane, count to three and then pull the rip cord. Leaping last from the training plane he passes all the others on the way down. They hear him saying as he shoots past "One-two, er. One-two, er. One-two, er…"

Meanwhile back at the Copper Beech in Baildon t`Con. Sec. war getting a bit aireated. On the stage Miss Doreen Golightly, singing for the price of her drinks, but makkin `eavy weather of "Velia oh Velia. My Witch of the Wood". The audience was chuntering on, knocking back its ale, crunching its chips, crumpling its bags and making like a civic banquet going down Browgate at fifty miles an hour. Doreen`s dulcet tones were drowned.

The Con. Sec. plugged `is mike into t`Amp. Just as Doreen`s `itting `er top note the room rang with the Con. Sec`s command, "Shut up the lot o`yer. Give t`poor cow a chance."

"Give t'poor cow a chance."

We do get down South from time to time to collect cups and such like for Soccer ant`Rugby League. Ah mind t`time a bus load o`lads fra Castleford went down to watch Cass win t`cup. Coach is finding its way back to Wallace Arnold land along Oxford Street when one o't' lads looks out an` yells, "Sitha there`s Seth Newman". Reet as rain, there`s old Seth, drunk as a posser `ead staggering along. They stop t`coach, grab Seth, an` after a long struggle drag `im back int`t Sharrah.

Off they go back ter civilisation. Three in the morning they`re back at Castleford hammering away at Seth`s door. No answer. For a quarter of an hour. No answer. Suddenly next door`s bedroom window shoots up. "Quiet yer noise" yells t`next door neighbour. "It`s no use `ammering for Seth at this time o`neet. Ee`s gone down ter London for t`week".

"It's no use 'ammering for Seth at this time o'neet."

Yorkshire born and Yorkshire bred – strong in t'arm and thick int' 'ead

Us Sayings

Yorkshire's sayings are the bridge between two worlds. The first is the Yorkshire that made them, and us: the world of Methodism and mills, chapels and coal, Liberalism and Labour, and the great town halls which were declarations of UDI. The second is today's pale province. Broad Acres of chapels and mills converted to des reses or art galleries, the back-to-backs pulled down, replaced by monuments to Poulson, and the cottages and barns of the Dales filled at weekends by commuters. It's enlarged, Greater Yorkshire with new added Humberside, and to that degree diluted. One world, warm and companiable, smokey and hard, proud and independent, is fading, to be replaced by another more glossy but less difficult (i.e. bolshy) and independent (i.e. bloody) minded because more dependent on and drained by the Great Wen of London but still recognisably Yorkshire. Our Yorkshire sayings are the continuity, the main umbilical link between them.

Yorkshire is, as Yorkshire says. Which is always in short order. We are basic, direct and honest, though a little inflexible or, as Elizabeth I's Archbishop of York put it in 1580, "a more stiff-necked, wilful or abstract people did I ever know". Our sayings are just the same because they're of our essence. No need to say more, to elaborate on the obvious or go in for language so flowery Alan Tichmarsh could have written it. We're the chosen people. We don't have to justify ourselves. Particularly not to ourselves. On the other hand, our judgements on others can be as critical as we want; always reduced to the few simple phrases necessary to tell them just how inadequate they are compared to us. It is after all for their own good.

We are what we say. Us is us sayings. Us sayings is us. They are the folk wisdom of the proudest people and the most important and best part of Britain where York was a capital when London was a swamp, its writ running the Roman world before London's reached Balham. Us sayings is our literature, our weltanschauung, our philosophy and what used to be our way of life. This is the first ever collection of Yorkshire sayings. The collected wisdom of God's Own County. Over 1,500 gems of wisdom, an amazing number from such a surly, taciturn lot. After all, Yorkshirefolk are folk of few words and most of those are "bugger off". We don't say much on the basis of the old adage that life is easier that way.

Yet thanks to this cautious cannyness everything we do say is bloody good sense: mirabile dicta, as they say in Harrogate. Wise. Cryptic. Boiled down to its essence and pithily put. So here they are. Read, learn and thoroughly digest. They don't make them like this any more.

No other county, country or even continent has so much wisdom to offer: Canada, with thirty one million people, has only 1,200 sayings and a mere 135 ways of saying "stupid", all set down in Cassalman's Canadian Sayings. Yorkshire's constitute a philosophy: the people's philosophy as Tony Blair might put it. Each defines something true in the Yorkshire experience and puts it with more eloquence than a paragraph of prose or a volume of poetry. So collected together they become the collective wisdom of the wisest folk around: the product of our folk and our history handed down to us by our ancestors via parents and the benign processes of growing up in Yorkshire homes, schools and neighbourhoods. They are something proud to look back at.

The Yorkshire phraseology may be antique - not many chapel 'at pegs around these days and few dolly pegs, while "two o'chips", an enormous quantity when fish were five pence and cakes tuppence halfpenny, would today be two chips and some scraps at two quid a packet. Yorkshire kids were called "clatter clogs long after they'd ceased to wear them (though I did - for a whole week), yet the perceptions and the sayings are eternal, an accumulated wisdom. Which is why it is important to set them down before the wisdom of generations of humanity's finest flowering is relegated to old people's homes, diluted to a meaningless mumble or driven out by the products of TV scriptwriters, political spin doctors, Clever Dick phrase-makers and the inrushing tide of globalisation and Americanisation. In France the Academie Francais would fight a bitter rearguard action. Here the Yorkshire Studies Department of York University isn't up to that job. So it has to be People Power as Yorkshire speyks to the world in its own language and lesser breeds without the county read, learn and thoroughly digest. It'll do them good.

Our sayings sum us up. They are us: of us, by us, for us. Not exactly generous, except with our advice for, and judgements on, other people, for there's no fault devoid of explanation. Shrewdly perceptive about faults, particularly those of others - witness the long sections on daftness, stupidity and other afflictions, right up to death. For we're a bit morbid but we're also self-sufficient, hard-working, diligent and honest. Never above making a bob or two on the side, of course that's what life's about. Above all, remember that the lesson from our sayings is that you can't fool us Yorkshire folk. We've got brilliant, built-in, fault finding and shit detection systems. Who was it vowed "We won't be fooled again?" Tykes won't be fooled the first time.

Yorkshire folk, like Yorkshire sayings, are the products of our industrial society. Life was hard, brass short, fun scarce. Yet struggle gives a shrewd perception of human weaknesses as well as a discipline and a sense of duty. Inevitably, therefore, the sections on faults, stupidity, incompetence and simple idiocy are as large as they are necessary. In those days every village had its idiot who needed neither vocational guidance nor an NVQ for the job. Villages had their cripples, the walking wounded of war and industry, their boozers and their deadbeats, and none were figures of fun. Just a feeling of "there but for the grace of God" and a warm support. After all there's a lot more daftness and a lot more faults outside Yorkshire than in it.

The reverse of this shrewdness is our pride in the county, its Broad Acres, and its inhabitants, i.e. us, though we're not exactly flowing with consolation for others without our advantages. Yorkshire folk are not naturally warm and sympathetic. Tea and sympathy are available (for a fee). But you'd do better paying for a psychiatrist or some other prostitute than coming to Yorkshire. All you'll get from us is a sharp delineation of your problems and prospects. Which will be helpful. But won't cheer you up. Hear what comfortable words our Saviour sayeth by all means, but remember, He's not from Yorkshire. Only his Father.

Us legacy is now threatened. Elocution teachers have tried in vain to stamp out the language but television and the

London media blandise, political correctness drives out colour and any mention of it. Yorkshire folk go south for work and a living and can't call a spade a spade, or anything but an optimised earth-moving hand tool, the internet offers no automatic translation or Tyke search engines and the Broad Acres are now broader as Greater Yorkshire - God's own region not county. It's a matter of duty to preserve the legacy, organise it and offer its full richness to the next generation. That will break the myth that it's Grim up North. It's not, it's colourful, vivid and better expressed than owt else.

Even worse, our uniqueness is under threat. The basic industries which shaped our way of life and gave us so much of our vocabulary and sayings shrink and fade as coal, steel, fishing and wool decline, communities and chimneys are pulled down, the great consumer society takes over and national media deluge and hose us down with alien cultures: London, Birmingham, Scotland and other lesser breeds without the county. So the saying production line slows and the colour and vividness of the product fades. It's not that they don't make them like this any more. But they don't make them this Yorkshire. Many of us like living in the past - life's cheaper that way - but not so many of us now speak it. Yorkshire had led the world in the production of Yorkshire phrases as well as wool and ours were the most graphic and colourful. In the twentieth century the production line broke. John Hartley died. Comedians went south and most TV soaps are about obnoxious folk so daft they live in the East End or Salford.

Yorkshire's accumulated folk wisdom must be preserved in its own right. Still living, no collection can be complete.

This is the work of one geriatric approaching senility who can't know it all, even if he's a Yorkshireman. Please help to add to the stock by telling us anything that's been missed for the next edition. Or indeed anything that's new, funny or worth preserving. Drop us a line or an email to the address on page 2. No C.O.D., of course. I'm a Yorkshireman after all. And don't be a dialect purist. My spellings and t't't' tutting aren't always consistant. But then I am a politician.

Incomplete though this first attempt at collecting Yorkshire's wit and wisdom may be, all can still benefit from it, women and outsiders more than Yorkshire men, but everyone concerned by the frivolity and shallowness of our modern world should heed it. The antidote to today's follies and fashions is the distilled, eternal, wisdom of the wisest folk on earth. That wisdom shaped our thinking and made us what we are today. Though purists flinch and philosophers sneer, we'll keep the sayings flowing here and those who ignore them do so at their peril. As the Keighley Kid, Alistair Campbell, might put it, they can go forth and multiply. Hopefully after buying the book. The rest of us can read, learn and inwardly digest, and use the sayings to awe and baffle folk outside Yorkshire. Enjoy. If tha dun't want thumping. But most of all be proud to bi Yorksher.

> *"Ah's open gobbed an' soft like*
> *Ah know more than ah tell*
> *The fella that wud bite me*
> *Will safe get bit hi'sel*
> *Ah's Yorkshire"*

Abuse

Did your mother have any children that lived?

Like a clown at a funeral

When tha wants to play I'll forget t'refrain

Thi village is missing its idiot

Anger

She's a temper in search of a tantrum

Ah'm that mad I could spit rust

A face as black as t'fire back

Ah'll 'ave thi guts for garters

Appearance

Sparrer shanks [thin legs]

Dressed like t'dog's dinner

Dressed up like two o'chips

Looking all roads for Sunday [cross-eyed]

As fat as a mawk [maggot]

She's like a bag o' bones

Ah'll drink thi beautiful

She's a face to stop a clock

So bald have seen better

Nivver judge a blade by t'heft [handle]

ANGER
Ah'll 'ave thi guts for garters

Awkward

Thi mam wants thi booits for loaf tins

Tha's worse ner a dog in a snicket

Ee's more taps ner nails

Tha frames nobbut badly

Tha's a reet clatterclogs

Blabber mouth

Tha jars mi earole

Tha could 'av knocked mi down wi' a foot o' sliver

A big tawker int a deep thinker

'Im as boasts he allus speyks 'is mind wudn't 'av much ter say if ee spoke nowt else

A gob as wide as t'Umber

Bellin an' bawlin'

She's allus sticking 'er fillings in

Ee babbles like Bradford beck

Tha knows some clog iron

A reet blatherskyte

Tha's full o'blackslavver

A reet slaver-bab

Nowt but a slobbergob

That's braidin it

She's allus kallin

More gob n'er brain

She'll gie thi some gob

Ee goes round bi Leeds an' Otley

She'd tawk t'ears off a donkey

She'll tawk yer 'ead off

Ee runs off at t'mouth like a soup sandwich

Ask him t'time o' day and he'll tell yer how to mek a watch

Empty vessels make t'most noise

Ee's full o' clog iron and twice as noisy

Booze

Tha's a soss pot [sometimes a 'reet soss pot']

A deal o' t'owd age pensions goes to support young publicans

A few jars wean't harm if tha dun't ower do it

Talk's cheap, but it teks money to buy whisky

Drunken men and childer speak the truth

Drink in, wits out

As drunk as a wheel head / a sweep / a fuzzock [= donkey] / a newt / a skunk

Drink's like a sack-tackle. It lifts a chap up to start wi but brings im dahn at t'finish. (John Hartley)

Tha can't preserve dignity in alcohol

*Drinkin ter drown yor sorrow is like cutting off yer tooa ter
cure a corn Ale weant work an' it weant laike quietly
awther*

It's a poor belly 'at can't warm a drop of ale

As dry as a lime-burner's clogs

Oft tha's made me friends mi foos
Oft tha's made me pop me cloas
But noa that thas so near me nose
Up tha comes an down tha goas

It's t'drink talking

Tha's an owd ale cart

*A stuttering king and a druffen queen [How the Misses
Murgatroyd next door used to describe George VI]*

As pissed as a newt

*And don't forget the gentle cries of closing time: "Sup up
an' gerrome", "T' rag's up", or, in the occasional upmarket
hostelry, "You hav been here too long for any good that
you are doing. Be gone and let us have done with you. In
the name of God go."*

Boredom

There's so little to do i' Eckmondwike we 'ad t'watch
t'Co-op bacon slicer

Miserable as a week o' wet Wednesdays

For summat lively we'd watch t'traffic lights change

We used to go to t'graveyard for a bit of excitement

It wor almost as slow as rigor mortis

Dead boring like necrophilia

Brass

It's capping sometimes what a ha'pence can do

A chap at doesn't care for brass may be goin to t'dogs

But a chap at cares for nowt but brass has gitten theer.
(John Hartley)

If tha want to lose a pal, lend 'im some brass

It's true at brass keeps goin' rahnd
An' noon but fouls would try to stop it
But what a chap would like t'know
Is hah to chase it rahnd an' cop it.
(Walter Hampson)

Ee chucks 'is brass around like a man wi no arms

When we say money is the root of all evil we mean other
fowk's money not ours

*Th' more brass a man gets an' th' more stuff ee puts in 'is
belly – an' the more a woman gets the more she puts on
her back*

Brass burns a hole in his pocket

Aye it's grand to ha' plenty o' brass (John Hartley)

If tha Bob dunt gee our Bob t'bob as thi Bob owes our Bob
our Bob'll gie thi Bob a bob on't nose

*Love of brass is t'root of half t'world's troubles
an' lack of it t'root of t'other 'alf*

Catch phrases (mostly from Yorkshire Comedians)

It's being so cheerful 'at keeps me going

The day war broke out, my missus said to me (Albert Modley)

Give 'im the money Barney

Ah'm proper poorly

Ah thowt "right monkey"

There's only them as knows their own knows

Can I do you now sir?

Ave a go Joe

Ah won't tek mi coat off. Ah'm not stoppin'

Na then Bradford. 'Ow are yer?

Don't forget the diver sir. Don't forget the diver

Titter ye not at the afflicted

Trouble at t'mill

Are yer courtin'?

TTFN – Ta Ta for Now

Get that effin ferret off me (Richard Whiteley)

CATCH PHRASES
TTFN – Ta Ta for Now

Cheer Up! (The consolations of Yorkshire philosophy)

To thi mind – peace
To thi heart – joy
To thi soul – strength
And courage, doy
May thi outgoings
Be nowt amiss
And thi home comings
Happiness

Mi father died at Wibsey tide,n left me all his riches:
A paper cap, a wooden 'at, a pair of leather britches,
A teapot wi'aht a spaht, a cup wi'aht a 'annel,
A bacca box wi'aht a lid, an; awf a tallaw cannel

Have a smoke o'your own if it's only as thin as a rat tail

It's better ner a slap int'face wi a wet haddock

A chap wi' peg legs nivver suffers wi' corns
It's 'ard what poor fowk mun put up wi
What insults and snubs they've to tek
Yct what little is to be expected
If a chap's a black coit on 'is back
As if cloos med a chap any better
Or good shooes improved a man's heart
As if muck in a suit smelled sweeter
Ner t'same muck wod smell in a cart.
(Walter Hampson)

Troubles as don't come are always worse than
t'misfortunes we 'av to face

Things is nivver as black as yar Nellie's doorstep

Tha'll clog ageen

Tek hod o' thissen

Mek t'best on't

Better than a poke in the eye with a sharp stick / a frozen mackerel

We're gradily weel off after all *(John Hartley)*

'Av a spell o' laikin

Class

As common as muck / as cheap as muck

If tha 'as nowt tha 'art nowt, if tha'd 'ad owt tha'd a been summat

Plenty blood but no suet

More pull than a canal horse

She reckons she's Lady Muck

Ah'm a member o' t' multitude who labour (John Hartley)

Ee'll only get to t'top o' t'ladder if 'is dad 'olds it up for 'im

Ee's a self-made man 'as worships 'is creator

She's as common as a door sneck wi no 'andles

Oo's ee when ee's at 'ome

Crafty

As leet geen as a posser head

As leet geen as a lodging house cat

Crooked bi nature is nivver made straight bi eddication

An ounce o' mother-wit is worth a pound o' clergy

Save your breath to cool your porridge

As straight as a woolworker's hook

Ee dropped out of Sunday School

Shake a bridle ower a Yorkshireman an' ee'll get up and steel t'horse

As crooked as a thirty bob note

That crooked ee dunt lie straight i' bed

Ee's one move ahead of t'bailiff

Straight as a dog's 'ind leg

Daft

Mad as a two bob watch

Tuppence short of a shillin'

Ther's nowt under 'is flat 'at

Daftness nivver built owt worth leaving up

As daft as a dish claht

If fowk weren't moastly fooils advertisers would starve

Ten pence t' t'shilling

Tha's not as daft as tha looks

As daft as a brush

A fooil's tongue is long enough to cut 'is own throit

Great clart 'ead

If tha brains were leather tha'd 'ave no shoes

DAFT
Ther's nowt under 'is flat 'at

Durst'o think we're med o'toffee

He's only got one oar in the water

Her lid's on too tight

Too daft to come in out o't'rain

Soft in t'ead

'Ee ladles water in a cullinder

As deep as t'Leeds-Liverpool canal

Ee don't play wi a full deck

'Ee's got bats in 'is belfry

Ten chips short of a pennorth

Some's born daft an' some 'as to work at it

Almost as daft as ee looks

Yer great dollop

Yer great cawf-ead

Slack set up

Funny as a fart in a bottle

'Is shuttle int' threaded

Ee's not got all 'is gubbins

As gaumless as a gooise

As sackless as a booat-'oss

Tha's a barm-pot

Daft as a pay cloise

Three sheets t't'wind

If it was raining soup he'd be stuck wi' a fork

Her mother dropped a few stitches when she knit 'er

As useful as a chocolate fender

Lame in t'brain

Ee wor gotten i' slack watter

As daft as a scuttle

Daft as Joe Bloggs dog 'at jumped in t'river to get out o' t'rain

My head will never save my feet

'Is lift doesn't go all the way to the top storey

'Is lift doesn't stop at all floors

Ee's two sandwiches short of a picnic

If brains were lard he wouldn't grease a pan

Two bricks short of a pallet

His driveway doesn't go all the way to the road / to the garage

He needs his attic rewired

He couldn't get a job as t'village idiot

His belt doesn't go through all t'loops

His receiver is off the 'ook

His stairs don't go all the way to the top

Nutty as a fruitcake with the fruit left out

Tha's got more boots ner brains

As cracked as a pot

Death

Dead as a door nail

As dead as a coffin nail

As dead as a hammer

Pop / cock yer clogs

His clapper's still, his trap is shut,
He says nowt, false nor clever,
He's no more use, nor mischief, but
His ear's to t'grahnd as ever!
James Gregson – 'Epitaph on a Politician'

She's in her pine overcoat

Descriptions

Slicker than hen poop on a pump handle

Flashy as a rat with a gold tooth

As fit as a fiddle

As deaf as a yat stowp

As deaf as a haddock

As 'ard as nails

He's got Brewer's Droop

As white as a ghooast

Ee waters t'lawn with beer so it comes up half cut

She's as changeable as t'weather

Not as green as it's cabbage-looking

So crooked he could hide behind a spiral staircase

His een stood aht like chapel 'at-pegs

He's so crooked, when he dies they'll have to screw him into the ground

Ee's reet well balanced wi' a chip on each shoulder

As bold as brass

Nobbut just a man

Ee's an auld misery guts

As fit as a lop

As leet as a cleg

As wick as a mop

As braan as a berry

Fame is a lump o' nowt inside a bubble

As busy as a cobbler's Monday

As thrang as a woman's tongue

As sick as a dog

As greedy as a fox in an 'en 'ouse

Stood like a stoup

As good natured as a pump

As sticky as glue

As strong as an 'orse

As long as t'parson's coat

As right as a trivet

As wet as a mill wheel

Ee keeps all 'is chairs at home

Wouldn't say boo to a goose

Short an' sweet like a donkey's trot

Talking to him is like pissing int' t'wind and trying not to get wet

He's so thin he has to stand in the same place twice, just to make a good shadow

Ee's enough to make a saint swear

Ee's that weak 'ee couldn't pull the skin off a rice puddin'

DESCRIPTIONS
He's got Brewer's Droop

Cunning as a Barnsley dog

A wooden church, a wooden steeple
Rascally place, and rascally people

Mutton done up to look like lamb

Mucky as a miner's arm pit

That bow legged as couldn't stop a pig in a snicket

Got a belly on 'im like a breeve's goit

Dim

As grey as a mowdiwarp [mole]

Ee's not the sharpest knife in the drawer

'Is brain's in 'is clogs

As thick as two short planks

Ee want there when brains were handed out

Ee's nobbut a gil in a pint glass

At back of t'queue for brains

For brains he's on t'minimum wage

As dim as a Toc H camp

Dim brains often go wi' nasty tongues

Tha can always tell a Lancastrian. But not much

Ee's a barge wi'out a rudder

Dirt

As nesh as us netty

Ee stinks like a pow-cat / pig / cow clap

As mucky as oor beck

A bit o' dirt nivver 'urt anybody

As mucky as a cow's bum

Mucky as a midden

Dustbin (unsorted)

(aka Miscellaneous Sayings, Perceptions and Yorkshireisms)

I had one of them but the wheel fell off

Rarer than hen's teeth

Dooan't forget t'owd fowks

T'pot calling t'kettle grimy behind

What's for tea besides nowt?

Nawther owt ner nowt

Exclamations

Ee by gum. We 'ad a reet fine do

Ah'll go ter t'top of our stairs.
[Yorkshire houses all had stairs to cram more houses on less land, to conserve the beauty of the county and make more money for landlords]

'Ells bells an' buckets o' blood

DUSTBIN (aka Miscellaneous Sayings)
What's for tea besides nowt?

EXERCISE
Ah'm fair knackered

Yer great clatter-can

I'll go to our 'ouse

Ah'm that flummoxed ah don't know

whether I need a shit, shave or 'air cut

Sod this for a game o' sodjers

Well ah nivver. Did yer ivver

That's peed on't' chips
[When Grimsby was a fishing port, Grimsby Town fans
would chant "We've peed on your fish"]

More bollocks ner a herd o' bullocks

Ah'm blowed

Ah'll gi'e thi what fo'

Ah'm furious fit to burst

Well ah'll go t' t' top ov our stairs

Exercise

Fair puffed

Fair payed

Ee's allus up at sparrow fart

Fair knackered

Exhortations

Gerronwiit

Giusabit

Giusummat

Giusago

Gius a kiss (trade up from then)

Giusbestovorder

Gerrout

Except Ye Repent Ye's addit

Goonwi'yer

Gerrin t' loony bin

Family

Their cat ran through our back yard

She's marrer tiv 'er dad [East Riding – looks like her father]

Only them as knows their own, knows

There's nowt war ner kids. Only more kids

Fidget

Thar't in an' out like a dog at a fair

As fidgety as a fly in a bottle

Buzzing about like a blue-arsed fly

Up and down like a toilet seat at Bowling Tide

Up and down like a whore's drawers

Like a flea on a fairy

Foibles

Ah unbethowt missen

As sour as a crab apple

Ah'd as life lig in bed

Ah'm fast for a bit o' band

Tha jars mi lugs

More chips ner 'Arry Ramsden

Them as sez they dun't like flattery is fishin' for it

Folk wisdom

If a bairn's teeath's odd, It'll seean gan ti God

A chap wi bad habits is called a good fellow

It's easier to find a fault ner to lose one

When a chap goes t' t'church ee's nivver short o' company

Fettle t'machine like it war thine

Men flatter thersens. Women like ter be flattered

As soon as a chap loves peace better ner ee loves truth there's an end to 'is usefulness

To a man 'at as wisdom folly is a relish

FOLK WISDOM
T'shoemaker's missus and t'smith's mare are allus worst shod

A wise man's ignorant o' things not worth knowing

The things yer see when you 'avn't got yer gun

Nowt more generous ner boxers.

Whenivver two on 'em meets each one tries to gie t''other more ner ee gets

Chop thi own wood an' it'll warm thi twice

We get what we deserve but only them at t'top admit it

T'shoemaker's missus an' t'smith's mare are allus worst shod

A good way to stop a chap's mooth is to keep your own shut. (John Hartley)

A chap 'at's liberal wi' t'advice is generally niggardly wi' 'is brass. (John Hartley)

There's some born fooils and there's some mek thersens fooils, an there's some get made fooils on. (John Hartley)

Few chaps believe all they ear sed, even when it's thersen 'at tells t'tale. (John Hartley)

Nivver boast about mekken a good start. It's t'finish 'at tells t'tale. (John Hartley)

When tha admits tha wor wrong yesterday tha's wiser today

Trying to look big meks thi small

Good sense is like a stream – t' deeper it is less t'noise

Closed lips an' open een save yer from many a fratch

Ther's noo cement been invented yet as can patch up a broken reputation

Nivver judge a man's worth bi t'length of 'is funeral procession: deeing may ha' been t'best thing ee ivver did. (John Hartley)

Dooan't think at because yo're one o'd't'rising generations as yer can luk dahn on them as lived befoor. Ya may a'ris'n but yer may 'av started very low down. (John Hartley)

What a chap gains bi study an' perseverance he oft pays doubly for bi 'is naybors' envy. (John Hartley)

Don't envy a feller because is dad 'as made 'im rich (John Hartley)

It's easier to find fault wi a chap for what ee's done, ner it is to show 'im ow ee should ha done it. (John Hartley)

Mek t'most o'thissen. It's all tha's got

A chap may change 'is cloos but ee doesn't change issen. A goois moults every year but it nivver becomes a swan. (John Hartley)

Life wi'aht fire is like summer wi'aht sun

Fowk are quicker to envy your success ner to pity your misfortune

The road to hell is paved wi' good intentions

If a chap could find a contented woman, a chap 'at nivver grumbles, a poet 'at's grown rich bi' 'is pen, a spendthrift 'at isn't in debt, a bonny lass 'at doesn't know it, an' a lad 'at isn't wiser than his fayther, he could start a museum

I believe it is to be wiser to believe in things 'at you cannot comprehend, ner to doubt all 'at yo' connot prove to be true

Best place for a picnic is allus further on

Shew me thi mates an' I'll tell thi'what thou art

Bi friendly to all but familiar wi' few

Fat sorrow is better na' lean sorrow

Worry is like a rocking horse: it gets thi nowhere

Fanned fire, and forced liver, nivver did well yet

A quiet conscience sleeps i' thunder

What is getten over t'devil's back is spent under 'is belly

It's adversity 'at brings prosperity.

It's havin' to feight 'at produces pluck.

This world is a big battlefield.

It makes thi' idle buckle tooth' modest becomes brave, an' th' upright win at th' finish.

Snivvelin' will nivver equal strivin'

A turn well done is soon done

Friendship that flames goes out like a flash

A wild goose ne'er laid a tame egg

To give some fowk too much help meks 'em 'elpless

Wilful waste brings woeful want

Friendship increases on visiting friends, but not if tha visits 'em too often

A black hen u'll lay a white egg

A chap wi' a new gold watch allus worries what time it is

It teks two ter fratch an' one to stop it

Politicians study wot 'as bin ter condemn it, what is ter upset it, and t'future for what they can get owt of it

If tha's puff to spare put it by, tha's need it on thi death bed

T'truth nivver 'urt anyone

Fine words butter no parsnips

A watched kettle nivver boils

Nivver prophesy unless tha knows (John Hartley)

Food

Eat like a Yorkshireman

There's nowt so quickly forgotten as meat an' drink

After t'cheese comes nowt

Wait-and-see pudding [said by the cook to inquiring children]

Masticate to a pulp

Ah'm 'ungry as a dog

Gerronwi'it

Put some lead in thi pencil

As nimble as a bookie's runner

Get agate

Get fettled

Shift thissen

Frame thissen

Get thi brat on and ger agate

Only a bad workman quarrels with 'is tools

Hackle thissen up

Good

Ee's no July Barber [not a fly-by-night]

A pocketful o' money an' a cellar full o' beer

That's reet gradely

Honest as t'day is long

Selling like spice

Ah get crankier an' wicker ivvery day

Gormless

Feckless folk are allus fain o' one another's company

Ee's like t'yeller line. Allus int'road

Ee's a clunterlugs [someone who keeps dropping things]

A reet clunter-head

Ee can't see for lookin' Bladder [can't do things in the right way]

Blether-'eead [empty head]

Ee'd be late for 'is own funeral

Gossip

Fain to be wick [glad to be alive]

Use tha brain more than tha wags thi tongue

Them as thinks t'least tawks t'most

Sh'telled t'tale from t'thread ter t'needle

Ee talks an' says nowt, an' ee's said nowt when ee's done

Knowing what tha says is better ner saying what tha knows

Greetings

Weer ta bahn?

Ah didn't awn yer

Nah then thee. 'Ow arta [Hello]

Ger out o' mi' road

Hopeless

As rare as rockin' 'orse droppins

Ee nivver lets 'is tea mash

God 'elp t'poor cow

Ee gi' us a ton o'nutty slack

He looks like summat that war sent for and didn't come

Her light's on, but there's nobody home

As weak as chip 'oil vinegar

Ee'll be a man afore 'is mother

Ee brought 'is pigs to a free market

Ee couldn't organise a piss up in a brewery

GREETINGS
Weer ta bahn?

Hunger

It's thi stomach 'at 'ods thi back up

Tha can't work wi'owt packing

Him 'at's etten more than he gradely should is awther greedy or empty

My belly thinks my throit's cut

'Unger's t'best sauce

Mi belly button's knockin' against mi backbone

Ah can eat two potatoes more ner a pig

'Is een are bigger ner is belly

Ah'd eet t'oven door if it were buttered

Illness

As ill as sooit an wesh

Lookin' a bit yonderly

Don't fret thissen

As ill as Owd Nick

Ah've got bellywak

As sick as Richard Whiteley's ferret

You look like death warmed up

'Is breakfast came back to see 'im

Insults

Yer great gobslatch.

Tha's a reet daft-ead / a reet toss pot / reet tosser

He's nowt a pound, an' bumpin' weight at that

Daft as a post / a brick / a stoop / a brush

He's only t'height of three pennoth o' copper

Tha'r't a parrot-faced wazzock

You must have been brought up in a tram shed (J.B. Priestley)

ILLNESS (including teeth!)
Don't fret thissen

IQ

(Low, Medium and Yorkshire)

For brains ee's baht

Lame int'brain

If 'is brains wor dynamite they'd not blow 'is cap off

Limp under t'cap

Kids

Childer suck their mother when they're young, an' their fayther when they're grown up.

A child an' a chicken is allus pickin'

It's easy to bury other folks' bairns

Nowt's gotten bi chance save kids

Know-alls

He's all talk an' says nowt

Too big for 'is booits / clogs

She's allus callin' an' tootin

*Some tawk becoss they think
they're born wi such a lot o' wit,
Some seem to tawk to let fowk
know they're born wi'owt a bit,
Some tawk in 'opes as what they say
may 'elp ther feller men,
But t'moast 'at trawk just tawk
because they like to hear thersen*

IQ (Low, Medium and Yorkshire)
If 'is brains wor dynamite they'd not blow 'is cap off

Know-nowts

If tha wants thi opinions respected keep 'em to yerssen

When a chap's nowther rich nor useful ee ought t'get wed. Somebody mun look after 'im.

Hod thi noise. If tha cannot tawke some sense keep tha mouth shut (John Hartley)

If tha wants ter believe all tha says say nowt

Lawyers

Fools an' obstinate buggers make lawyers rich

If you want to be poor goo to law.

Win or lose, it maks varry little difference

Justice is blind but she in't deaf, an' 'im 'at can jingle t'moast brass oft wins t'case.

A case in't cellar's worth two in't court

Ee lies like a lawyer

Lawyers are t'only fowk who can work in sewers but nivver stink

Lazy

As idle as a Ludlam dog at leans its 'ead agint wall ter bark

Ees that idle ee thinks manual labour's a Spanish socialist

Ee likes work so much he could sit and watch it all day

There's more work in an asprin

As lazy as a ladder at leans agin t'wall

Ee'll only turn ower t'garden in 'is mind

Lies

As big a lier as Tom Pepper an' he were pawsed aht o'hell three times afore breakfast for lying

He lies like a dirty rug

Liar, liar, pants on fire

Ee's nivver been introduced tert'truth

Lonely

Ee's a pot o' one [solitary, withdrawn, independent]

I couldn't warm to thee if we were cremated together

As lonely as a milestone

Ee only likes 'is own company

Meanness

Ee's got short arms and long pockets when it comes ter paying

A deal o' fowk gooa regular to a place a worship but if some on 'em only gets as much religion as they pay for. Ahm feared it in't much   (Ben Preston)

Ee chucks is brass around like a man baht arms

As graspin' as a toll bar

As tight as a damp clothes line

As mean as a cat wi a mouse

T'chap at boasts ee owes nowt to nabdy won't be 'appy if ee means ee didn't intend to pay owt to anybody (John Hartley)

Weak tea = watter betwitched and tea begrudged

Ee's that mean eed split a current in two

Ee wouldn't part wi't' drips off 'is nose

Ee's that tight ee won't let 'is teeth chatter when ee freezes.

Ee's that mean ee wouldn't pee on yer if yer war on fire

That mean ee won't give yer t'time o'day

If thou wants ta know t'value of a pound, try an' borrer one

Ee wouldn't tell yer tomorrow wa' Sunday if yer didn't know

Charity begins at home in Yorksher and usually stays there

Keep yer 'and on yer ha-penny

It costs too much and a half

Ee gives a gill for t'price of a pint

There's no pockets i'backless neetgahns

He's lower than a snake's belly

He'd sell an anchor to a drowning man

She's so tight she'd squeeze a penny until the queen cried

He's so mean, he wouldn't give you t'drips off his nose

Ee wouldn't part wi't'reek of 'is own muck

Misery and misanthropy

Come back again when tha' can't stay so long

We wipe t'sweat off us brow wi t'slack of us bellies

Nivver do nowt for noabody

Ah reckon nowt to it

As mawngy as an owd cat

As solemn as a coo

Things are that bad even them as nivver pays in't buying

Moods and states

Ah'm sad flayed [I'm scared]

Ah'm fair capped

Bloss up   [Brighten up]

Tha mun gan a dee [Go away or drop dead]

As dry as a booan

As blind as a bat

As thick as inkle weyvers [narrow tape worm or narrow loom]

As greedy as a rake

As snug as a bug in a rug

As fat as a mowdiwarp [mole]

As edgy as a crocodile in a handbag factory

As deaf as a pooast

As waik as a kittling

Mardy as a cat

On mi' beam ends

A pot o' oil [withdrawn; aloof]

Ah'm reet mawky [looking sickly]

Doan't let's get narky   [bad-tempered, sarcastic]

Up Dicky's meadow [in difficulties]

Muck

Mucky as a duck puddle

As sure as a louse in Pomfret

Weer there's muck there's brass

As mucky as a pig sty

She's wedded t' t'midden for sake of t'muck

Tha's like 'orse muck, allus in't road

Ee's allus in 'is muck

Mucky as a midden

Mum (sayings mi mam sed to us)

Patience is a virtue. Find it where you can.
Seldom in a woman and nivver in a man

You make a better door than a window

Tell the truth and shame the Devil

MUCK
Like 'orse muck – allus in t'road

Better to be ten minutes late in this world than ten years early in the next

Hard work never hurt anyone

Little birds in their nests agree [we never did]

How much did you pay for it?
"Money and fair words"

Idleness is nothing unless it's well followed

Don't be backward in coming forward

Handsome is as handsome does

Naughty

Tha's marrer to Bonny [ie Bad as Napoleon]

Tha's war ner our Kate

As straight as a shopping trolley

As cunning as a cart load o' monkeys

Old Age

There's many a good tune played on an old fiddle

At seventeen a feller thinks hissen a clever man
At twenty-five ee knows ee's got a world reforming plan
At forty ee admits ee didn't larn soo much at schooil
At sixty he's just larnt enough to knaw ee's bin a fooil
(Walter Hampson)

An old nowt will nivver be owt

Them at's same age as me is allus older

I'm as old as my tongue and a little older than my teeth

There may be snow on the roof, but there's still fire in the furnace

Age is when tha needs a rest afore bed

A new broom sweeps clean but an old 'un knows t'corners

As old as Methusalah an' twice as dead

Some folk only behave thersens when they're too old to do owt else

Optimism **(a rare virtue)**

A breet smile drives away a deep shadow

Ah'm reet champion

Ah'm reet grand

Mi whippet can give a rabbit three times round t'cellar an' cop it easy

Overworked

Ah'm reet thrang

As throng as Throp's wife when she hanged hersen wi t'dish claht

Up to 'er een i'work

Ah'm working an tewin fr' morn to neet

Perseverance

Keep t'band in't nick

Allus hod on

Hod thi whist

Nivver say nivver

Nivver say nay

Nivver say nowt

Pessimism (a conditioned reflex)

Old Abe's pig didn't weigh as much as ee expected it would. An' ee allus thowt it wouldn't (Walter Hampson)

Gie nowt for owt

Yer nivver know oo yer friends are

Nice view but it weant pay t'rent

Ah've been / seen wahr

Nobbut middlin'

Can't say owt's up [but ah would if ah could]

Mustn't / Can't grumble [ditto]

Philosophy

If it wearn't for summat there'd be nowt

Summat's better ner nowt

If a man thinks ee's well off ee's well off

Angels nivver av whiskers

This an' better might do, but this an' worse 'll nivver do

Awlus be at t'foor end of a feast an' t'latter end of a fight

One tale's good 'till another's told

Cop t'lot an' stick [motto of the Yorkshire Altruism Society]

Pudden's pudden [Italian Che sera sera]

There's nowt gotten in an 'urry but chance brats

You can't grow grass on a busy street

PHILOSOPHY
Ther's nowt good bowt cheap

After three days both fish and guests start to stink

There's more ways ner one to skin a cat

Maggie, tha'rt bonny,
As bonny as onny;
Mi sovereigns are few
An' mi maisters are monny;
But whahle Ah can weyve,
An' whahle tha can spin,
Well keep trouble aht,
An' happiness in.
(William Beaumont)

Everyone reaps as ee sows except ont'allotment

A bit o' help is worth a deal o' pity

A weddin', a woo,
a clog an' a shoe,
A pot full o' porridge
an' away they go

Good folk are scarce, tek care on 'em

Go a borrowin', go a sorrowin'

Tha mun't ever be t'main man at a weddin' or a funeral

Anyone wi't use of is een can see

Ther's nowt good bowt cheap

Physical characteristics

As slow as a snail / as a stutterer

As lame as a three-legged dog

As tough as leather

As tall as t'mill chimney

As hoarse as a raven

As wet as t'dish cloot

As soft as putty

As tired as a dog

As full as an egg

Lanky like a cloos prop

A case of brewer's goitre

A belly built int' pub

Places

'Alifax is built of wax
'Eptonstall o' stone
In 'alifax ther's bonny lasses
In 'eptonstall ther's nooan

Said the Devil flyen ower 'arrogate's wells:
"Ah think am 'ome by t'smells"

The muse in Tadcaster can find no theme
But a most noble bridge without a stream

The verse before on Tadcaster was just,
But now great floods we see and dirt for dust.

Lincoln was, London is, but York shall be
The greatest city of the three

Oxford for learning, London for wit,
Hull for a woman, and York for a tit

Slowit, weer they raked t'moon aht o't' watter

PLACES – Hutton Rudby
Far more rogues than honest men

Slowit, weer they put t'pigs on t'wall ter listen t' t'band
[also said of Marsden and Milnsbridge]

Pudsey, weer t'ducks fly backwards,
ter keep t'muck aht o'theer een
Pudsey, weer they've all bald heads
cos they pull 'em aht o' t'pit wi' suckers

Proud Pudsey, poor people, High Church and low steeple
Ossett, weer they black-leaded t'tramlines

When Roseberry Topping wears a cap,
Let Cleveland then beware a clap [downpour]

Ther's more laikes ner works i'Barnsla

Bradford for cash,
Halifax for dash,
Wakefield for pride and poverty;
Huddersfield for show,
Sheffield what's low,
Leeds for dirty and vulgarity.

Castleford women must be fair
Cos they wash in t' Calder an' sind in t' Aire

From Hell, Hull and Halifax, Good Lord Deliver us

When all the world shall be aloft
Then Hallamshire shall be God's croft

Hutton Rudby, Entrepen
Far more rogues than honest men
Great Kelk where God never dwelt
And honest man never rode through it

They put a wire fence round Kippax to keep t'fog aht

Selby was a seaport town
When Goole was but a marsh;
Now Goole it is a seaport town
And Selby fares the worse.

There's Hunt Pot and Hull Pot,
Jingle Pot and Joggle Pot;
A cave without a bottom,
An' another at's deeper still

Wharfe is clear, and Aire is lythe,
Where the Aire drowns one,
Wharfe drowns five
Blood thirsty Dee each year
needs three,
But bonny Don, she needs none
The shelvin', slimy river Don
Each year a daughter or a son.

Ainderby Steeple
Where there are more rogues
Than honest people

Barton for sartin;
Twea churches and nivver a parson

Borrowby Hills an' Newton Broos
Them's t'spos for hosses an' coos.

When Dighton is pull'd down,
Hull shall become a great town

Market Weighton
Robert Leighton;
A brick church
And wooden steeple,
A drunken priest
And a wicked people

Marrick church is seen the best
Just as the sun withdraws to rest
A Scarborough warning:
A word and a blow
But the blow first.
Semerwater rise, Semerwater sink,
And swallow all the town

But this lile house
Where they gave me meat and drink
Sutton boiled mutton,
Brotherton beef,
Ferrybridge bonny lasses
and Knottingley thief

Play it down (Be Yorkshire)

Summat an' nowt

Nawther mickle nor muckle

More tops ner noils

Owista? Nobbut awfish or Nobbut nazzard [neither well nor ill]

Better ner yesterday war ner t'morn

'Appen it is, 'appen it in't

Better ner like [a good day]

That's summat like [OK]

Ah'm nobbut fair ter middlin

Least said soonest mended

Poverty

Friday flits
Have not long sits

If tha wants ter be poor stay int'pub John Hartley

He bears poverty ill who's ashamed on it

Nowt's for nowt

Baht 'owt. Ah'm baht

Ee ant got two ha'pennies for a penny

Ee lives in't' pop shop

Goin dahn t'nick

So poor ee couldn't buy a ticket to a free lunch

Poverty poverty knock
Mi loom is saying all day
Poverty poverty knock
Gaffer's too skinny to pay
But ah know ah can guttle
When ah 'ear mi shuttle
Go poverty poverty knock
(Thos. Sykes Daniel 1889-1970)

Tha' clam'd an' hauf damned mi lad, still tha' t a deal
nearer heaven nur some (John Hartley)

Proverbs

A steady income meks many folk unsteady

Blessed is t'bride at t'sun shines on
An' blessed is t'dead at t'rain rains on

There's allus t'most thrustin weer there's t'least room

A dimple in the chin brings a fortune in
A dimple on the cheek leaves the fortune to seek

Free advice is only worth its cost

A cobweb i't'kitchen
An feeat marks on t'step
Find noa wood i't'yewn

An' neoa cooals i't'skip

There's nowt like tryin'

T'nearer t'home sweeter t'meeat

Talk o't'devil an' yer'll 'ear is clogs

There's allus room at t'top but none to sit down

A chap wi' a barrel of ale int'cellar nivver wants for company

It's a lot better / cheaper / nicer to live int'past

Life's warp comes throo Heaven, t'weft's fun bi us sen (John Hartley)

Queer (all senses)

More camp ner a row o' Boy Scout tents

Ther's nowt so queer as fowk

As queer as Dick's 'at band

All t'world's queer except thee and me – and tha's a bit

A reet lad-lass [stolen by Arnold Schwarznegger, who calls opponents "girly-men"]

Happy as a bugger playing rugger

As queer as a currant bun

A daft 'awpence

Rag Bag

**(a.k.a. Miscellaneous or Odds an' Sods
or Owt 'at fits nowhere)**

Put t'wood in't oil [My father. In extreme cases he would shout "Were you brought up in a barn?]

Ah'm sad flayed [I'm scared]

Gerrup t'wooden steps to bed (or climb t'wooden 'ill)

Yan, tean, thethera, methera, pimp [Ancient Celtic sheep count – not much used since the Celtic sheep died off]

Reputation

Have a name to get up early, an' tha' can lie i'bed all day

Ee's nobbut a gill in a pint pot

Gie a dog a bad name

Sage advice

Say nowt to nobody about nowt i' no road

Wisdom is ignoring what's not worth knowing

'Ear all. See all. Say Nowt (Of course!)

Ate All. Sup all. Pay nowt

Best way to cheer thissen up is to cheer someone else up

*It"s not them 'as knows most that 'av t'mooast ter say
Nor is it them 'as 'av mooast that give mooast away*

It'll save thi no small trouble

If when speaking tha teks care
Of whom tha speyks to whom tha speyks
And how and when and where

Get thi brain an' thi' gob inter gear

Tha these them as these thee, an' tha dunt them as dunt

*Temperance means health – good grub, brass i'th'pocket,
a fair name – happy hooam, thrivin' bairns – a clear heeard
– an' a breet prospect for hereafter*

Better give a shillin' than lend hafe a craan

Borrowed garments nivver sit weel

Good luck goes to some more than it should but seldom
more than they want

*Give a child while he craves, an' a dog while 'is tail wags,
you'll 'ave a fair dog, but a poor child*

Them 'at never knew pain preach patience

*Neither build thissel up, nor pull thissel down. If tha builds
thissel up nubdy 'ull believe thee; an' if tha pulls thissel
down, they'll believe a lot more than tha says*

If thou wants a good servant, tek neither a relation nor a
friend

Thou doesn't deserve sweet, if thou willent taste sour.

Him that does thee an ill turn will never forgive thee

*If when yo're doing yer best, th' clouds o' misfortun'
surround yer, nivver heed! Keep straight on.   Th' moon
shines on, no matter what clouds obscure it, an' when they've
passed looks breeter nor ever.*

A good cow can 'av an ill cawf

A bridle for thee tongue is a necessary piece o' furniture

Moderation's fine if tha dunt ower do it

Nivver put a drum set in a back-to-back

Don't snag [spit] in t'ash trays. Ah want t'tabs for missen [sage advice shouted by Commissionaire at t'bug hole (a.k.a. Pavilion Cinema), Shipley, at children's matinées]

If ther's a lot, eat a little. If there's a little, eat it all

It teks less time to do summat for folk ner to explain why tha didn't

Them as buys happiness gets poor value for t'brass

Sayings

If tha Bob dun't gie our Bob t'bob
as thi Bob owes our Bob our Bob'll
gie tha Bob a bob on't nose

If tha knows nowt say nowt.
If tha knows summat say nowt

Of tools" "It's that sharp tha could
ride bare arsed to Donny on it"

Doan't fash thissen. Tha's got all t'time there is

Self-sufficiency

If tha wants owt done well, do it thissen

If tha wants summat interesting, talk to thissen

If a job's worth doing, it's worth doing well

If at furst tha don't succeed, ask thissen why

If at first tha don't succeed, do summat else

Sex

She's t'town bike

She's showing more meat than t'butcher's window

Busy as a Hull harlot

Gi'up Gi'ower Gerremoff Gerroff
[South Yorkshire mating call]

Tha's bin tom cattin'

Put 'er t' t'tup

Them as weds weer they don't love
mostly loves weer they don't wed

Lads love is lassies' delight,
And if lads don't love, lassies will flite.

Yer don't look at t'mantelpiece when yer poking t'fire

She lays more ner our 'ens

She goes like a train / tram /steam engine

Ah wouldn't kick 'er out of bed

A bachelor nivver meks t'same mistake once

Single chaps are content wi one woman. Until they get 'er

A chap 'ats allus smilin' an' smirkin' at ivvery woman is
soon to be wed

Ee's an awd tup

Sex when tha's old is nobbut tatty watter

As wick as a weasel, kittling, lop, etc

Ee's got summat under 'is brat

Tha'll nivver miss a slice off a cut cake

No 'arm in another spoonful once t'lid's off

She's up t'spout / got a bun in't'oven

Show-offs

Ther's many a showy gown covers a mucky shift

We're all Adam's children, but silks an' satins maks the difference

Better go to heaven i'rags ner to hell i'embroidery

She thinks she's summat but she's nowt

As toff as owd 'Arry

All mouth and trousers

Ee's a reet mee maw (mee mo)
[person with affected behaviour]

Shut Up

Od thi wisht

Od thi din

Shut thi cake oil / gob

If silence is golden tha's banked

Giusbestovorder: Shurrup

Stupid (including Southerners)

Tha talks like an 'alfpenny book baht leaves

Tha knows little an' does less

It's easier to convince a philosopher ner it is to win an argument wi' a fooil (John Hartley)

'Is 'ead'll nivver save 'is legs

Ee asn't enough sense to come in out of t'rain

As gaumless as a lot o' throttled earwigs

It's a sackless fooil at's allus grinning   (John Hartley)

Ee's leet weight, on nowt a pund

You can tell fowks from 'Arrogate but you can't tell 'em much

Tha's a speed bump on the information highway

He was toilet-trained at gunpoint

Stupid as the day's long

So stupid, when you say 'ello, ee's stuck for an answer

If brains were vinegar she couldn't have enough to pickle an egg

As dim as a Toc H lamp

She's not got every pan on t'oven

THUMPS
Ah'll clip thi lugs

Thumps

Fighting like ferrets in a sack

Fratchin's better ner feytin

Sh' fotched 'im a claht

Twelt	}	
Thrash	}	
Fetch 'im one	}	*To hit*
Flay	}	*(Prohibited*
Bray	}	*for children*
Thump	}	*up to 45)*
Wallop	}	
Hammer	}	

I'll wall thi 'een up

Ah'll clip thi lugs

Reet poshing

Ah'll belt thi into t'middle of next week

Gie 'im a bunch o' fives

Tits

Does ta want a medal or a chest to pin it on?

As flat as a witch's tit

Get yer tits out for t'lads

Yer don't get many of them to a pound

As flat as a yard o' pump watter (Not Jordan)

Toasts

'Eer's to me an' mi wife's 'usband, not forgetten missen

Eer's ti us an all or us. May we nivver want for owt. None on us. Ner me neither

The Lord be thanked for what we're getting,
If ther'd been more to ate ther'd 'ave been more etten

Them as ates t'most puddin gets t'most meat

God bless us all an mek us able
Ter ate all t'stuff 'at's on this table

Mek a lang airm. To a guest at a meal, help yourself and no asking

Fear God. Honour t'King, eat the porridge an 'od thi din

Here's tae thee and thine
Nat forgettin me and mine
When thee and thine meet me and mine
May me and mine be as good to thee and thine
As thee and thine's been to me and mine

'Ear all see all say nowt
Ate all sup all pay nowt
An if tha 'ivver does owt for nowt
Do it for thissen

Nah cum mi lad, fill up thi glass
We'll drink t'Yorkshire great in brass
Happier wi every passing year
T'brass gets less but t'great's still there

From witches an' wizards an' long-tailed buzzards
an' crazy things that run in hedge bottoms,
Good Lord deliver us.

Ere's ter me, An mi wife's usband. Not forgettin missen.

Trust no one

Phony as a nineteen bob note

He'd steal owt but a red-hot stove

Them as gives nowt gets nowt

Ah'd trust 'im as far as ah could throw 'im

Ugly

She can't 'elp being ugly but she could 'av stayed at 'ome

She looks as if she tossed a sparer an' lost

Ee's a face like a busted clog

She's got one eye on't pot an' another on't chimney

As plain as a pikestaff

Ee in't bald – ee's shorter ner is 'air

Glasses like pop bottle bottoms

A face like t'back end of a bus

An 'ead like a set pot

As bald as a blether o'lard

Bat-lugs

Four-eyes

As thin as a lath

Ah've seen better 'air on bacon

Smiling like a cracked piss pot

Got a grin like a butcher's dog

A smile like a wave in a slop pail

Red as a spanked baby's bum

She fell in't'rag bag and got out dressed

He's got friendly eyes: they're allus lookin' at each other

When t'wind changes tha'll stay like that

UGLY
Seen more 'air on a coconut

She's as pretty as a bald-faced heifer

Seen more 'air on a coconut

She's a used car with a new paint job

He's so ugly that when he was born the doctor slapped his mother

She was so ugly she got a job as a test pilot in a broom factory

All fur coat an' no knickers

Untidy

Ah'm in mi'muck

Ah've got 'ands that feel like Dick's feet

All over t'shop

Tidy as a tip

Neat as a netty

Useless

Tha' mind's like a shop: no use if it's closed

As much use as a chocolate fireguard

Tha can educate some folk till they're daft

As handy as a duck wi a muck fork

All tha' gets from a pig is t'grunt

As useless as a man made o' band

WEATHER
I'Eptonstall when t'wind snaps they all fall over

Ee couldn't 'it t'barn door sat ont'sneck

As useless as a chocolate teapot

As much use as casters on a crutch

Useless as tits on a bull

As much use as a pocket in a shroud

Tha great clod hopper

Tha's a waste o' space

Useless as a ten bob watch

Wealth

Better go to heaven i'rags, ner to 'ell i'embroidery

It int wat tha 'as as meks yer 'appy but things yer doan't as meks yer miserable

Them as 'as, gets

It's nobbut three generations from clogs to clogs

A chap wi' a metal watch is nivver feared o'pick-pockets

Ee 'as brass comin' out o' 'is ears

Charity begins at 'ome i'Yorkshire and usually stays there

Weather

For every fog i'March, there'll be a frost i'May

Deean't cast a cloot, Till May bi oot

Ya moan't wesh blankets i' May,
Or else ya'll wash yer soul away

Happy is the bride the sun shines on
Blessed is the corpse the rain falls on

I see t'mean an' t'mean sees me
God bless t'sailors oot on t'sea

Onion skin
Very thin
Mild weather coming in:
Onion skin thick and tough
Coming winter cold and rough

The first cock of hay, Frights the cuckoo away

It's silin i'stair rods

It's goin ter sile it down

It wor sleetin' bad enough to tek pleasure out of a buryin'

If the cock crows going to bed
He'll certainly rise with a watery head

As cold as Christmas

If it rains 'afore seven, it'll be fine 'afore eleven

A peck o'March dust, an' a shower i'May,
makes corn green, an' t'fields gay

The east wind is too lazy to blow round you, it goes
straight through

A mackerel sky not varry long wet not varry long dry

A green Christmas maks a fat churchyard

More raan, more rust

It's looking black over our Will's Mother's [it's going to rain]

Ossin ter slart [it's starting to rain]

If tha dunt like us weather 'ang on.
There'll be some more along

That cold folk 'ave their 'ands in their own pockets

Raan raan faster. T'bull's int'pasture

Raan raan go away. Cum agaan another day

I'Eptonstall when t'wind snaps they all fall ower

Fine weather's not allus t'best

Wed

(and other states of misery, not including Gay partnerships or livin' ower t'brush – or ower t'latch)

When everything goas wrong wi' a chap an' ee cannot lay t'blame on 'is wife 'is marriage is a failure

When a cook gets wed she's nivver any dripping for sale

Livin' tally, ower t'brush

A ring round yer fingers is worth two round yer een

Nivver put yer 'usband on a pedestal, 'Eel nobbut want dustin'

*It's a good horse at nivver stumbles,
an' a good wife as nivver grumbles*

Hot tongue and cold shoulder for tea

Faults are thick where luv is thin

When a plain woman weds she dunt invite 'er beautiful sister to live

Tha needs a wife or an allotment

Many a rich bachelor meks a poor 'usband

Nivver luv brass but allus luv weer brass is

Marry in Lent – tha'll live to repent

More belongs to marriage than four bare legs in a bed

Lasses want nowt but husbands, an' when they 'ave 'em, they want ivverything

A chap cannot thrive who 'as a wasteful wife

It's not every couple as meks a pair

Every lass can keep house better than her mother, 'til she tries

When poverty comes in through t'door, love flys out 'at winder

There's more gets wed na does well

Sam Smith's livin' wi a single woman

Ee couldn't find a double woman 'at ud 'av 'im

Afore they're wed ee can't live baht 'er. After ee can't live wi 'er

When tha wife's quiet nivver ask 'er ter do owt – she's enuff ter do to put up wi' thee

Women

(also incoporating bags, bints, birds, slags, slappers, slatterns, slovens, sluts, talent, tarts,trollops and tosspots)

Only one thing's more changeable ner a woman an' that's two

A woman o' thirty sez she's twenty-five but when she's sixty she'll boast o' seventy

She's allus chewing t'bacon

Single chaps are content wi' one woman. Until they get 'er

As flat as a yard o' pump watter
Ya cannot mak' ale wi'out watter
Nor Yorksher Pud baht batter
But a feller needs nowt t'mek
trouble an' strife
If ee lives wi 'is mother-in-law
an' 'is wife (Walter Hampson)

Gie a woman an inch an' she reckons she's a ruler

Be wary be chary
Tek heed who tha courts
Ther's lasses i'plenty
I'sahzes n' sorts.
But if tha's be happy
Tek on wi a lass
At's nimble wi't' thimble
An' careful wi't brass.
(Rhymes in the North Country Humour, 1971)

Sympathy's what tha' mun give a woman to get t'full story

Never tell a Yorksher lass tha's not worthy on 'er.
Let 'er find out for 'ersen

She's allus chewin' t'cud

What should a lass learn afoor getting wed? Learn to play
t'pianner or ha to mek a dress; but learn to mek a pie first.
That's t'promise to keep   (John Hartley)

*Nivver blame a lass for spending 'er brass on a stylish
bonnet. It may be a means o' grace. She's pretty sewer to
attend t'chapel regular for a Sunday or two (John Hartley)*

A bonny young lass is varry charmin' but a nice old woman
is still sweeter an' more soul satisfyin'

A dog's nose and a maid's knees are allus cowld

If time ivver comes when all men are brothers, then all th'
wimmin will be sisters, an' that'll be awkward

*Women are a disagreeable lot.
When two on em fall aht, which
ever comes to tell you abaht it,
it's allus t'other one to blame
Walter Hampson*

Ter mek 'omes dearer
An' dark skies clearer
An' bring 'eaven nearer
Is women's work (John Hartley)

If tha's looking for a perfect woman, gi' ower. She's deead.

Ther's nowt meks a woman as mad as 'aving a saycret
nobody wants ter know.

A woman's tongue wegs like a lamb's tail

She'd start a fight in an empty house

She was pure as the snow but she drifted

She's narrower than hen's eyes

Homely as a row of back-to-backs

Work

Workin' for little is better ner laikin

*'Ard work nivver killed anyone /'urt anyone / did anyone
any 'arm*

Twist an' turn, reel an wind
Keep a contented mind

Life's all bed an' work

If tha dunt work tha dunt eat

Nivver heed. It'll come to Saturday

Work's fascinating. Ah can watch fowk doing it for hours

*A collier lad a collier lad
A collier lad for me O
He works in a hole as black as t'coal*

And brings all 'is brass 'ome to me O
West.Riding mining ballad from
(A.L. Lloyd, Come all ye bold miners)

There's no time off when tha's nowt ter do

Mining: A job for life (NCB adverts, 1970)

Ah tew on tool all day fer nowt

Better to work ner to fret

Better sit idle ner work for nowt
Ther's t'meat hung dahn afor t'fire to roast
Ther's t'pudden on t'brondee afore it ta toast
Potatoes top o't' hop, they'll be done enif souin
But ah think tha can weave a few more bobbins bi nooin
(John Bromley – White Rose Garland, 1947)

Work's that good for thi, tha's best leaving some of it til
tomorrow

Working on a dead 'orse [doing work already paid for]

If ya miln pieces reit
An ya cuttle'em streit
An finish em fit for to wear
Then your wage sud be good
An your work sewerly sud
Not leave ya o'en burdened wi' care (Ben Turner)

Nivver grummel becos yer've got to work: a lazy chap is
nivver happy. (John Hartley)

If yer could get all yer want for th' axin for yer'd goa to
work for t'pleasure on it John Hartley

'Ard work nivver killed anyone – but t'thowt on it's killed
thousands

Nivver buy owt wi' a wooden handle – it allus means hard
work

Gurt tawkers are seldom gurt workers

Gi' us some bulwark   [extra effort]

Tha dunt mek footprints on't'sands o' time sat on thi bum

Yorkshire (including best, biggest, beautiful, bounteous, brilliant and bloody good)

Eat like a Yorkshireman

Don't speak t'Queen's English – It's t'Queen's Yorksher tha needs

Tha's not from round 'ere

A day can't sooart all a Yorkshireman
Wun at's was nur sum bud not much
(John Hartley)

As Yorkshire as they mek 'em

Yorkshire's hills and moors,
Lancashire's mills n' hoors

Yorkshire watter: too wet to walk on, too dry to drink and allus in short supply

Yorkshire born and Yorkshire bred.
Strong in t'arm an' thick int' 'ead

If tha can't tawk sense to a Yorkshireman then say nowt an' shut thi gob.

An offcumden 'll nivver mek a Yorkshireman

Shake a bridle ower a Yorkshireman's grave an' ee'll rise an steal t'orse